Caring and Capable Kids

A Character Curriculum for Teaching Respect, Responsibility, Kindness, and Self-Control

Linda K. Williams
Dianne Schilling
Susanna Palomares

INNERCHOICE PUBLISHING

Illustrations: Zoe Wentz and Dianne Schilling

Copyright © 1996, Revised, 2010, Innerchoice Publishing • All rights reserved
ISBN – 10:   1-56499-067-9
ISBN – 13:   978-1-56499-067-9

Experience sheets, stories and song lyrics may be reproduced in quantities sufficient for distribution to students in classrooms and groups utilizing Caring and Capable Kids activities. All other reproduction by any means or for any purpose whatsoever is explicitly prohibited without written permission. Requests for permission should be directed to INNERCHOICE PUBLISHING.

Dedication

To Thomas Pettepiece

1944-1995

Tom, the dearest of friends and a caring, supremely capable colleague, edited the original edition of Caring and Capable Kids, published in 1989. He contributed four stories to that version, all of which appear in this book as well. Tom dedicated his entire life to peace and a portion of his legacy is represented by his accomplishments in global education, communications, and as a national board member of the U.S. committee for UNICEF. Our loss is softened knowing Tom's peace is complete.

Rejoice!

What others are saying about *Caring and Capable Kids*...

Recently our school district decided to get back to some basic character building. I was looking everywhere attempting to get information that was timely and easily used throughout my school. There were many programs out there to choose from but none quite as concise and personal as this. These lessons are exactly what I need to help motivate my teachers. As an administrator I want teachers to access information that is useful and easy to find. This book has become a big loaner. You can never have too much information on kindness, tolerance, self-control and responsibility. This book has it all.

    Muriel Bartolini,
    Elementary Vice Principal

This book is so wonderful!! The items selected for each lesson are easy to understand and reproduce. There are times when I need to work with a group of students and no preparation time is allotted. The lessons in this book are ready to go at a moments notice. They are fun, up-to-date and active for students. I recommend that every Guidance Assistant and Counselor have one of these books on the shelf or in your carry bag. Just do it.

    Penny Clark,
    Elementary Guidance Assistance

Now, more than ever, our children need to be empowered to make a difference in the world. Caring and Capable Kids, is a collection of lessons, stories, and songs that captures the essence of establishing a healthy self in order to be of service to others. Today's children ARE members of a global society. They can and will influence the world – this book gives children a foundation for how to take strong character into action.

    Deanne Rohde,
    Principal,

We all want to do what we can to instill in our children those values, virtues, and skills that will bring success, love, and fulfillment into their lives, and we know we need to impart this kind of personal wisdom to them beginning when they are young. Caring and Capable Kids is a beautifully thought out and imminently useful guide for teachers who are touching young minds.

    Judith Hand, Ph.D.
    Biologist, Author, Peace Ethologist
    Founder, AFutureWithoutWar.org

This book proves to be a valuable tool in the enrichment of character development in children of all ages. A must have in any educator, parent or teacher's library!

    Julie P. Harris
    Magnet Coordinator/Media Production

Contents

Caring and Capable Kids 1

An Introduction to Sharing Circles 4

Kindness 13

Tolerance 37

Respect 59

Service to Others 79

Responsibility 95

Self-Control 121

Peer Pressure 143

Ethical Decision Making 163

Caring and Capable Kids:

Caring and Capable

Compassionate and Competent

Concerned and Skillful

Charitable and Resourceful

Humane and Adept

Empathizing and Actualizing

A child growing in exquisite balance. We may be setting our sights immoderately high, but that's what we're after. As teachers and counselors, that's what all of us want.

And why not? Every child is an unwritten symphony of emotional and cognitive intelligences — a potential masterpiece of unique skills and talents with plenty of empathy for others.

We have designed this book to help you make this vision a reality, by offering a collection of diverse, immediately usable instructional tools. As an educator on the front lines, you already possess the desire, the commitment, and the expertise to create caring and capable kids. What you need are strategies and activities. This book provides excellent group strategies and over seventy-five fully developed activities.

What Constitutes a Caring Kid?

Caring is an outgrowth of empathy. Empathy is the ability to know how another feels, to have an emotional affinity for another's experiences, to take another's perspective.

In his best-seller, Emotional Intelligence (Bantam, 1995), Daniel Goleman points out that the roots of empathy form as an infant experiences attunement with parents and other caregivers. Attunement is a type of feedback in which a parent demonstrates understanding of what the infant is experiencing. Attunement goes beyond imitation. A coo is answered not just by an echoing coo, but by a combination of verbal and nonverbal cues that both reflect and add to the original "message." Teachers and counselors who use the skill of active listening with school-age children (and teach them to listen actively to each other) are demonstrating a verbal version of the same skill. An active listener doesn't merely parrot, an active listener paraphrases words while mirroring feelings to demonstrate real understanding.

Anyone who has taught children to use active listening knows that possessing a measure of empathy is a prerequisite to mastering the skill. Furthermore, empathy comes more easily to children with higher levels of self-awareness and emotional intelligence—children who can identify, accept, and verbalize their own feelings and thoughts, and recognize how those thoughts and feelings lead to behaviors.

Having empathy allows children to understand the feelings, thoughts, and actions of others. Effectively taking the perspective of others makes it possible to care.

Caring children are to varying degrees loving, empathic, respectful, compassionate, helpful, and nurturing. Caring children demonstrate concern for their own condition as well as that of others, and they also care what happens to the environment.

Last, but not least, the caring child is developing important core moral values. In, Educating for Character (Bantam, 1991), psychologist and educator Thomas Lickona states that good character consists of "knowing the good, desiring the good, and doing the good — habits of mind, habits of heart, and habits of action." In other words, a morally mature person knows what is right, cares deeply about what is right, and does what is right.

Our caring child cares deeply about what is right.

Characteristics of a Capable Kid

The passion and compassion of the caring child might never be transformed into good deeds or coupled with intellectual abilities to accomplish great things without skills and competencies. Capable is the responsive side of the equation — the productive channeling of empathy and other caring emotions into responsible action.

A capable child is learning to exert self-control, restrain impulses, postpone gratification, express anger appropriately, and use emotion to guide effective effort.

A capable child is responsible, honors commitments, keeps promises, and practices age-appropriate skills associated with goal setting, thoughtful decision making, and peaceful conflict resolution.

Capable children know how to evaluate and, if necessary, resist peer pressure. They are learning to make ethical decisions, to measure the possible effects of alternative choices on themselves and others, and to choose the course of action that leads to the greatest good. They can distinguish right from wrong, and are learning to judge right from "more right," and wrong from "more wrong."

Caring and capable is a combination that can't lose. For this activity guide, we've expanded each of the two C's into four key developmental areas and designed activities to build understanding and skills in each.

Caring:	**Capable:**
Kindness	Responsibility
Tolerance	Self-Control
Respect	Peer Pressure
Service to Others	Ethical Decision Making

Perspective-taking is a feature of many of the stories and activities in this book and Sharing Circles are an excellent venue for practicing listening skills.

This activity guide provides you with many effective, enjoyable aproaches to cultivating caring, capable kids.

How to Use the Activities

As outlined previously, the activities in Caring and Capable Kids are grouped into eight developmental areas or units. The first four expand the concept of caring. The second four focus on skills and competencies related to the concept of being capable.

The activities within each unit are arranged in a logical sequence. However, in most cases you are not required to implement them in the order presented. All of the activities are completely independent and capable of standing on their own.

Modifications to activities should be made to suit the ages, ability levels, cultural/ethnic backgrounds, and interests of your students. Suggested adaptations for younger students are included at the end of several activities; however, you will know best how to maximize the appropriateness and impact of each experience, so please take those liberties.

The Stories

The first component of each unit is a short story that embodies the unit theme. Depending of the reading levels of your students and your collective preferences, these stories may be read to the students or duplicated and distributed for individual reading or small group read-arounds. Several discussion questions follow each story. Use these to facilitate an exchange of reactions to the story, examination of the dilemmas and choices faced by characters in the story, and the meaning of the story in general. Always review the questions in advance and adjust them to suit the readiness of your students to deal with various concepts.

The Experience Sheets

Following each story is an "experience sheet," which you may duplicate and distribute to your students, giving them an opportunity to respond personally to the story and to write about similar situations that they have faced in their own lives. Have the students complete their experience sheets either in class or as homework. When time allows, invite the students to share their answers to the questions in small groups. This is an excellent way to help the students further internalize the concepts presented in the story and unit as a whole.

Throughout the units, additional experience sheets follow certain activities. Directions for the use of these handouts are always outlined in the activity itself.

Discussion Questions

At the conclusion of every activity, you will encounter another list of "Discussion Questions." Discussion questions are provided to help you involve students in thinking about and summarizing the learnings derived from a particular activity. They promote thoughtful reasoning, the use of higher-level thinking skills, and internalization of knowledge and skills. Use any or all of the discussion questions provided, and feel free to ask your own questions. When planning for implementation, always allow plenty of time for debriefing and discussion.

Song Lyrics

As a final component of each of the units, song lyrics that relate to the theme of the unit have been included. These songs provide a particularly effective and enjoyable way of reinforcing the lessons. Music is included with each unit because it activates students mentally, physically, and emotionally, and is a known way to improve memory content and detail. The music to accompany each song is available as a download from www.songsforteaching.com, an online educational music store. You can also choose to create your own tune or have your students create the music to accompany the lyrics. The words can also be read as a poem.

Sharing Circles

Following the story and accompanying experience sheet, the first two activities in each unit are Sharing Circles. A Sharing Circle is a small-group discussion characterized by a unique two-part structure (sharing followed by summary discussion) and prescribed rules of conduct that ensure acceptance, listening, safety, mutual respect, and confidentiality.

The Sharing Circle is an extremely powerful process for the development of empathy, effective listening, self-control, and many other targeted skills. Part of its value for this purpose lies in the fact that it is guided by an established procedure and a specific topic. In addition, the process requires that students demonstrate respect, responsibility, trust, caring, and fairness as a condition of participating in every circle.

If you are new to Sharing Circles, please read the following section of this book thoroughly before leading your first one.

An Introduction to Sharing Circles

The Sharing Circle is a unique small-group discussion process in which participants (including the leader) share their feelings, experiences, and insights in response to specific, assigned topics. Sharing Circles are loosely structured, and participants are expected to adhere to rules that promote the goals of the circle while assuring cooperation, effective communication, trust, and confidentiality.

The character traits and skills needed to be both caring and capable develop largely within a social environment. The nature of the Sharing Circle environment — the messages it sends to students and the behaviors it encourages and discourages are highly conducive to their development. Students follow clear rules of conduct, accept ownership of those rules, are supportive of one another, and experience a sense of satisfaction by complying with the guidelines and procedures of the circle. Regular implementation of Sharing Circles can noticeably accelerate the development and internalization of the qualities and skills addressed in this book.

To prepare yourself to take full advantage of the Sharing Circle process, thoroughly read and digest the portions of this section that deal with the Sharing Circle rules and procedures.

All Sharing Circle topics are intended to develop awareness and insight through voluntary sharing. This occurs in the first (or sharing) phase of the circle. The discussion phase of the circle, for which specific questions are provided, allows students to understand what has been shared at deeper levels, to evaluate ideas that have been generated by the topic, and to apply specific concepts to other areas of learning.

The topic elaborations provided under the heading, "Introduce the Topic," are guides for you to follow when presenting the topic to your students. They are excellent models, but need not be read verbatim. The idea is to focus the attention of students on the specific topic to be discussed. In your elaboration, try to use language and examples that are appropriate to the age, ability, and culture of your students.

Developing Empathy

As students follow the rules and relate to each other verbally during the Sharing Circle, they are practicing respectful listening and oral communication. As they listen carefully while other students ponder and discuss the various topics, the children have repeated opportunities to mentally take the perspective of others. They are also required to demonstrate awareness and control over their own feelings, thoughts, and behaviors during the circle. Through the positive experience of give and take, they learn the importance of interacting responsibly and effectively.

The Sharing Circle topics offered in this book address many qualities inherent in caring along with important skills that make a person capable — keeping agreements, developing responsible habits, solving problems, demonstrating respect for self and others, being loyal, being trustworthy and honest, following rules, demonstrating kindness and consideration, resolving conflicts, etc.

Topics like these help students identify core moral values, and they require students to describe incidents and behaviors from their own experience that illustrate those values.

The Sharing Circle allows students to confront difficult decision-making situations. In response to the topics posed, students are asked to state positions, to think about their reasons for selecting those positions, and to listen to the positions and reasoning of others.

Learning Right from Wrong

As students learn to relate effectively to others, issues related to acceptable and unacceptable behavior surface again and again. Students learn that all people have the power to influence one another. They become aware not only of how others affect them, but of the effects their behaviors have on others.

The Sharing Circle process has been designed so that healthy, responsible behaviors are modeled by the teacher or counselor in his/her role as circle leader. Also, the rules require that the students relate responsibly and effectively to one another. The Sharing Circle brings out and affirms the positive qualities inherent in everyone and allows students to practice effective modes of communication. Because Sharing Circles provide a place where participants are listened to and their feelings accepted, students learn how to provide the same conditions to peers and adults outside the circle.

The Sharing Circle teaches cooperation and promotes caring. As equitably as possible, the circle structure attempts to meet the needs of all participants. Everyone's feelings are accepted; everyone's contributions are judged valuable. The circle is not another competitive arena, but is guided by a spirit of collaboration. When students practice fair, respectful interaction with one another, they benefit from the experience and are likely to employ these responsible behaviors in other life situations.

Practicing Responsible Behaviors

One of the great benefits of the Sharing Circle is that it does not merely teach young people about interpersonal interaction, it lets them interact! Every Sharing Circle is a real-life experience of social interaction where the students share, listen, explore, plan, and problem solve together. As they interact, they learn about each other and they realize what it takes to relate effectively to others. Any given Sharing Circle may provide a dozen tiny flashes of positive interpersonal insight for an individual participant. Gradually, the reality of what constitutes effective behavior in relating to others is internalized.

Through this sharing of interpersonal experiences, students learn that behavior can be positive or negative, and sometimes both at the same time. Consequences can be constructive, destructive, or both. Different people respond differently to the same event. They have different feelings and thoughts. The students begin to understand what will cause what to happen; they grasp the concept of cause and effect; they see themselves affecting others and being affected by others.

The ability to make accurate interpretations and responses in social situations allows students to know where they stand with themselves and with others. They can tell what actions "fit" a situation. Sharing Circles are marvelous testing grounds where students can observe themselves and others in action, and can begin to see themselves as contributing to the good and bad feelings of others. With this understanding, students are helped to conclude that being respectful and responsible towards others feels good, and is the most valuable and personally rewarding form of interaction.

How to Set Up Sharing Circles

Group Size and Composition

Sharing Circles are a time for focusing on individuals' contributions in an unhurried fashion. For this reason, each circle session group needs to be kept relatively small—eight to twelve usually works best. Once they move beyond the primary grades, students are capable of extensive verbalization. You will want to encourage this, and not stifle them because of time constraints.

Each group should be as heterogeneous as possible with respect to sex, ability, and racial/ethnic background. Sometimes there will be a group in which all the students are particularly reticent to speak. At these times, bring in an expressive student or two who will get things going. Sometimes it is necessary for practical reasons to change the membership of a group. Once established, however, it is advisable to keep a group as stable as possible.

Length and Location of Circles.

Most circle sessions last approximately 20 minutes. At first students tend to be reluctant to express themselves fully because they do not yet know that the circle is a safe place. Consequently your first sessions may not last more than 10 to 15 minutes. Generally speaking, students become comfortable and motivated to speak with continued experience.

In middle-school classrooms, circle sessions may be conducted at any time during the class period. Starting circle sessions at the beginning of the period allows additional time in case students become deeply involved in the topic. If you start circles late in the period, make sure the students are aware of their responsibility to be concise.

In elementary classes, any time of day is appropriate for Sharing Circles. Some teachers like to set the tone for the day by beginning with circles; others feel it's a perfect way to complete the day and to send the children away with positive feelings.

Circle sessions may be carried out wherever there is room for students to sit in a circle and experience few or no distractions. Students can sit in chairs or on the floor. Some leaders conduct sessions outdoors, with students seated in a secluded, grassy area.

How to Get Started

Teachers and counselors have used numerous methods to involve students in the circle process. What works well for one leader or class does not always work for another. Here are two basic strategies leaders have successfully used to get groups started. Whichever you use, we recommend that you post a chart listing the circle session rules and procedures to which every participant may refer. Sharing Circle rules can be downloaded from www.InnerchoicePublishing.com.

1. Start one group at a time, and cycle through all groups. If possible, provide an opportunity for every student to experience a circle session in a setting where there are no disturbances. This may mean arranging for another staff member or aide to take charge of the students not participating in the circle. Non-participants may work on course work or silent reading, or, if you have a cooperative librarian, they may be sent to the library to work independently or in small groups on a class assignment. Repeat this procedure until all of the students have been involved in at least one circle session.

Next, initiate a class discussion about the circle sessions. Explain that from now on you will be meeting with each circle group in the classroom, with the remainder of the class present. Ask the students to help you plan established procedures for the remainder of the class to follow.

Meet with each circle session group on a different day, systematically cycling through the groups.

2. Combine inner and outer circles. Meet with one circle session group while another group listens and observes as an outer circle. Then have the two groups change places, with the students on the outside becoming the inner circle, and responding verbally to the topic. If you run out of time in middle-school classrooms, use two class periods for this. Later, a third group may be added to this alternating cycle. The end product of this arrangement is two or more groups (comprising everyone in the class) meeting together simultaneously. While one group is involved in discussion, the other groups listen and observe as members of an outer circle. If you like, invite the members of the outer circle to participate in the review and discussion phases of the circle.

What To Do With the Rest of the Class

A number of arrangements can be made for students who are not participating in circle sessions. Here are some ideas:

- Arrange the room to ensure privacy. This may involve placing a circle of chairs or carpeting in a corner, away from other work areas. You might construct dividers from existing furniture, such as bookshelves or screens, or simply arrange chairs and tables in such a way that the circle area is protected from distractions.
- Involve aides, counselors, parents, or fellow teachers. Have an aide conduct a lesson with the rest of the class while you meet with a circle group. If you do not have an aide assigned to you, use auxiliary staff or parent volunteers.

- Have students work quietly on subject-area assignments in pairs or small, task-oriented groups.
- Utilize student aides or leaders. If the seat-work activity is in a content area, appoint students who show ability in that area as "consultants," and have them assist other students.
- Give the students plenty to do. List academic activities on the board. Make materials for quiet individual activities available so that students cannot run out of things to do and be tempted to consult you or disturb others.
- Make the activity of students outside the circle enjoyable. When you can involve the rest of the class in something meaningful to them, students will probably be less likely to interrupt the circle.
- Have the students work on an ongoing project. When they have a task in progress, students can simply resume where they left off, with little or no introduction from you. In these cases, appointing a "person in charge," "group leader," or "consultant" is wise.
- Allow individual journal-writing. While a circle is in progress, have the other students make entries in a private (or share-with-teacher-only) journal. The topic for journal writing could be the same topic that is being discussed in the Sharing Circle. Do not correct the journals, but if you read them, be sure to respond to the entries with your own written thoughts, where appropriate.

Leading the Sharing Circle

This section is a thorough guide for conducting Sharing Circles. It covers major points to keep in mind and answers questions which will arise as you begin using the program. Please remember that these guidelines are presented to assist you, not to restrict you. Follow them and trust your own leadership style at the same time.

Steps for Leading a Sharing Circle

1. Welcome Sharing Circle members
2. Review the Sharing Circle rules*
3. Introduce the topic
4. Sharing by circle members
5. Ask discussion questions
6. Close the circle

*optional after the first few sessions

1. Welcome Sharing Circle members

As you sit down with the students in a Sharing Circle group, remember that you are not teaching a lesson. You are facilitating a group of people. Establish a positive atmosphere. In a relaxed manner, address each student by name, using eye contact and conveying warmth. An attitude of seriousness blended with enthusiasm will let the students know that this Sharing Circle group is an important learning experience—an activity that can be interesting and meaningful.

2. Review the Sharing Circle rules

At the beginning of the first Sharing Circle, and at appropriate intervals thereafter, go over the rules for the circle. They are:

> **Sharing Circle Rules**
>
> 1. Everyone gets a turn to share, including the leader.
> 2. You can skip your turn if you wish.
> 3. Listen to the person who is sharing.
> 4. There are no interruptions, probing, put-downs, or gossip.
> 5. Share the time equally.

From this point on, demonstrate to the students that you expect them to remember and abide by the ground rules. Convey that you think well of them and know they are fully capable of responsible behavior. Let them know that by coming to the Sharing Circle they are making a commitment to listen and show acceptance and respect for the other students and you. It is helpful to write the rules on chart paper and keep them on display for the benefit of each Sharing Circle session.

3. Introduce the topic

State the topic, and then in your own words, elaborate and provide examples as each lesson in this book suggests. The introduction or elaboration of the topic is designed to get students focused and thinking about how they will respond to the topic. By providing more than just the mere statement of the topic, the elaboration gives students a few moments to expand their thinking and to make a personal connection to the topic at hand. Add clarifying statements of your own that will help the students understand the topic. Answer questions about the topic, and emphasize that there are no "right" responses. Finally, restate the topic, opening the session to responses (theirs and yours). Sometimes taking your turn first helps the students understand the aim of the topic. The introductions, as written in this book, are provided to give you some general ideas for opening the Sharing Circle. It's important that you adjust and modify the introduction and elaboration to suit the ages, abilities, levels, cultural/ethnic backgrounds and interests of your students.

4. Sharing by circle members

The most important point to remember is this: The purpose of these Sharing Circles is to give students an opportunity to express themselves and be accepted for the experiences, thoughts, and feelings they share. Avoid taking the action away from the students. They are the stars!

5. Ask discussion questions

Responding to discussion questions is the cognitive portion of the process. During this phase, the leader asks thought-provoking questions to stimulate free discussion and higher-level thinking. Each Sharing Circle lesson in this book concludes with several discussion questions. At times, you may want to formulate questions that are more appropriate to the level of understanding in your students—or to what was actually shared in the circle. If you wish to make connections between the topic and your content area, ask questions that will accomplish that objective and allow the answering of the discussion questions to extend longer. We have left a space on each page for you to note significant other questions that you create and find effective.

6. Close the circle

The ideal time to end a Sharing Circle is when the discussion question phase reaches natural closure. Sincerely thank everyone for being part of the circle. Don't thank specific students for speaking, as doing so might convey the impression that speaking is more appreciated than mere listening. Then close the group by saying, "This Sharing Circle is over," or "OK, that ends our circle."

More about Sharing Circle Procedures and Rules

The next few paragraphs offer further clarification concerning circle session leadership.

Who gets to talk? Everyone. The importance of acceptance in Sharing Circles cannot be overly stressed. In one way or another practically every ground rule says one thing: accept one another. When you model acceptance of students, they will learn how to be accepting. Each individual in the circle is important and deserves a turn to speak if he or she wishes to take it. Equal opportunity to become involved should be given to everyone in the circle.

Circle members should be reinforced equally for their contributions. There are many reasons why a leader may become more enthused over what one student shares than another. The response may be more on target, reflect more depth, be more entertaining, be philosophically more in keeping with one's own point of view, and so on. However, students need to be given equal recognition for their contributions, even if the contribution is to listen silently throughout the session.

In most of the circle sessions, plan to take a turn and address the topic, too. Students usually appreciate it very much and learn a great deal when their teachers and counselors are willing to tell about their own experiences, thoughts, and feelings. In this way you let your students know that you acknowledge your own humanness.

Does everyone have to take a turn? No. Students may choose to skip their turns. If the circle becomes a pressure situation in which the members are coerced in any way to speak, it will become an unsafe place where participants are not comfortable. Meaningful discussion is unlikely in such an atmosphere. By allowing students to make this choice, you are showing them that you accept their right to remain silent if that is what they choose to do.

As you begin circles, it will be to your advantage if one or more students decline to speak. If you are imperturbable and accepting when this happens, you let them know you are offering them an opportunity to experience something you think is valuable, or at least worth a try, and not attempting to force-feed them. You as a leader should not feel compelled to share a personal experience in every session, either. However, if you decline to speak in most of the sessions, this may have an inhibiting effect on the students' willingness to share.

A word should also be said about how this ground rule has sometimes been carried to extremes. Sometimes leaders have bent over backwards to let students know they don't have to take a turn. This seeming lack of enthusiasm on the part of the leader has caused reticence in the students. In order to avoid this outcome, don't project any personal insecurity as you lead the session. Be confident in your proven ability to work with students. Expect something to happen and it will.

Some circle leaders ask the participants to raise their hands when they wish to speak, while others simply allow free verbal sharing without soliciting the leader's permission first. Choose the procedure that works best for you, but do not call on anyone unless you can see signs of readiness. And do not merely go around the circle.

Some leaders have reported that their first circles fell flat—that no one, or just one or two students, had anything to say. But they continued to have circles, and at a certain point everything changed. Thereafter, the students had a great deal to say that these leaders considered worth waiting for. It appears that in these cases the leaders' acceptance of the right to skip turns was a key factor. In time most students will contribute verbally when they have something they want to say, and when they are assured there is no pressure to do so.

Sometimes a silence occurs during a circle session. Don't feel you have to jump in every time someone stops talking. During silences students have an opportunity to think about what they would like to share or to contemplate an important idea they've heard. A general rule of thumb is to allow silence to the point that you observe group discomfort. At that point move on. Do not switch to another topic. To do so implies you will not be satisfied until the students speak. If you change to another topic, you are telling them you didn't really mean it when you said they didn't have to take a turn if they didn't want to.

If you are bothered about students who attend a number of circles and still do not share verbally, reevaluate what you consider to be involvement. Participation does not necessarily mean talking. Students who do not speak are listening and learning.

How can I encourage effective listening? The Sharing Circle is a time (and place) for students and leaders to strengthen the habit of listening by doing it over and over again. No one was born knowing how to listen effectively to others. It is a skill like any other that gets better as it is practiced. In the immediacy of the circle session, the members become keenly aware of the necessity to listen, and most students respond by expecting it of one another.

In the Sharing Circle, listening is defined as the respectful focusing of attention on individual speakers. It includes eye contact with the speaker and open body posture. It eschews interruptions of any kind. When you conduct a circle session, listen and encourage listening in the students by (1) focusing your attention on the person who is speaking, (2) being receptive to what the speaker is saying (not mentally planning your next remark), and (3) recognizing the speaker when she finishes speaking, either verbally ("Thanks, Shirley") or nonverbally (a nod and a smile).

To encourage effective listening in the students, reinforce them by letting them know you have noticed they were listening to each other and you appreciate it. Occasionally conducting a review after the sharing phase also has the effect of sharpening listening skills.

How can I ensure the students get equal time? When circle members share the time equally, they demonstrate their acceptance of the notion that everyone's contribution is of equal importance. It is not uncommon to have at least one dominator in a group. This person is usually totally unaware that by continuing to talk he or she is taking time from others who are less assertive.

Be very clear with the students about the purpose of this ground rule. Tell them at the outset how much time there is. When it is your turn, always limit your own contribution. If someone goes on and on, do intervene (dominators need to know what they are doing), but do so as gently and respectfully as you can.

What are some examples of put-downs? Put-downs convey the message, "You are not okay as you are." Some put-downs are deliberate, but many are made unknowingly. Both kinds are undesirable in a Sharing Circle because they destroy the atmosphere of acceptance and disrupt the flow of discussion. Typical put-downs include:

- overquestioning.
- statements that have the effect of teaching or preaching
- advice giving
- one-upsmanship
- criticism, disapproval, or objections
- sarcasm
- statements or questions of disbelief

How can I deal with put-downs? There are two major ways for dealing with put-downs in circle sessions: preventing them from occurring and intervening when they do.

Going over the ground rules with the students at the beginning of each session, particularly in the earliest sessions, is a helpful preventive technique. Another is to reinforce the students when they adhere to the rule. Be sure to use nonpatronizing, nonevaluative language.

Unacceptable behavior should be stopped the moment it is recognized by the leader. When you become aware that a put-down is occurring, do whatever you ordinarily do to stop destructive behavior. If one student gives another an unasked-for bit of advice, say for example, "Jane, please give Alicia a chance to tell her story." To a student who interrupts say, "Ed, it's Sally's turn." In most cases the fewer words, the better—students automatically tune out messages delivered as lectures.

Sometimes students disrupt the group by starting a private conversation with the person next to them. Touch the offender on the arm or shoulder while continuing to give eye contact to the student who is speaking. If you can't reach the offender, simply remind him or her of the rule about listening. If students persist in putting others down during circle sessions, ask to see them at another time and hold a brief one-to-one conference, urging them to follow the rules. Suggest that they reconsider their membership in the circle. Make it clear that if they don't intend to honor the ground rules, they are not to come to the circle.

How can I keep students from gossiping? Periodically remind students that using names and sharing embarrassing information is not acceptable. Urge the students to relate personally to one another, but not to tell intimate details of their lives.

Kindness

Story:

Four Eyes and Brace Face
Experience Sheet

Sharing Circles:

*A Time I Felt Sorry For Someone Who Was Put Down
Something I Did to Make Someone Feel Good
A Time I Made Friends With a New Kid*

Activities:

A Book of Kindness
Writing and Art Activity

Kindness Makes News
Current Events Research

The Kindness Link
An Ongoing Recognition Project

Kindness Coupons
A Writing and Design Project

Kindly Correspondence
Letter Writing and Discussion

Song/Poem:

Handle with Care

Four Eyes and Brace Face
by Beverly Ward Trust

"Boy, that sister of mine!" Scott grumbled, checking his watch again. "School's been out for fifteen minutes now and still no sign of her! She's becoming 'Miss Popularity' and I'm becoming 'Mr. Ex-Baseball Player.' If I'm late for one more practice, Coach Calen will..."

Out of the corner of his eye Scott saw Heather and her two friends running excitedly up the hill.

"Scott!" Heather called, panting for breath, "Quick! You gotta come with us!"

"Do you know what time it is?"

"I know I'm late, Scott, I'm sorry, but we've got something to show you — quick!"

"Heather, I've got baseball practice!"

"I know, Scott, this will only take a minute. You've gotta see this. Come on," Heather shouted, grabbing her brother's hand and dragging him down the hill with her two friends.

The four of them raced past the school office, down the steps and out onto the playground where several children were playing after school. They stopped at the jungle gym. Heather, Janet, and Sally started giggling.

"Look, Scott!" Heather exclaimed. She pointed to a line of children waiting for a turn on the jungle gym.

"What am I supposed to be looking at?" He growled, feeling embarrassed at being in the middle of a group of giggling girls.

"Over there!" the three girls chanted. "Don't you see him?"

"See who?" Scott shouted.

"Wait a minute, he's just about to turn around. Okay... look, Scott, right there — the boy in the blue shirt."

At that moment a little boy in a blue shirt turned around. He looked normal enough from the back, but when he turned around, Scott saw that the boy had braces. Not only braces, but the full head gear.

"So this is why I'm late for baseball practice?" Scott asked.

"Did you ever see anything so weird?" Janet snickered, "He looks like something from outer space!"

"Yeah, Scott, a real space creature," Heather laughed.

"Who is he?" Scott asked.

"He's the new boy in our class — or the new space creature I should say," Heather quipped.

"His name's Raymond," Sally said, "but everyone calls him BRACE FACE."

"Yeah, BRACE FACE FROM OUTER SPACE!" the girls shouted.

By this time the three girls were laughing so hard they were holding their sides. The little boy in the blue shirt could hear their laughter and knew they were laughing at him. Slowly, he turned his head, picked up his lunch box, and walked away.

"Well, that's great girls, I hope you're proud of yourselves!" Scott said.

"What do you mean, Scott? We thought this was something you wouldn't want to miss," Heather said.

"Well, you were wrong! I've got better things to do than hurt somebody's feelings," Scott replied. "Like baseball practice!" And with that he turned and left.

"What's the matter with him?" Janet asked.

"I don't know, but I've got to go. See you tomorrow," Heather called as she ran to catch up with her brother.

The next morning, Heather, Sally, and Janet dashed to their desks just as their teacher was greeting the class.

"Good morning, boys and girls, who would like to do the attendance this morning?" Ms. Miller asked. Several hands went up. "Well, let's see, let's have someone new today. Would you like to, Raymond?"

"You mean BRACE FACE!" some voices blurted out from the back of the room. And with that, the whole class burst into laughter. Raymond was so embarrassed he threw his hands over his face and raced out of the room.

Ms. Miller turned to the class and demanded to know who had called out the name. She looked over a sea of seemingly innocent faces. "I can't believe that someone in this classroom has forgotten our most important rule," she said.

"Didn't we agree that we would treat others like we would like them to treat us? Well, someone here has treated Raymond very badly, and I'd like to know who that person is!"

Ms. Miller scanned every face. In the back of the room, three red-faced little girls were trying very hard to look normal. Both Janet and Sally nervously denied any guilt. "Heather, were you the one?" Ms. Miller asked. Heather could feel all the eyes in the classroom fixed right on her. The room was absolutely silent. She looked up at Ms. Miller painfully, as she considered the consequences of doing something wrong. Reluctantly, she whispered, "Yes, M'am, it was me."

"Well, Heather, I am certainly disappointed in your behavior. I'll see you after school today and we'll write down what happened in a letter to your parents."

Heather peeked up. "Yes, M'am," she whispered.

After school that day it was a long, nerve-wracking ride home. All the way home Heather worried about what her parents were going to do.

After dinner Scott asked, "When are you going to show the letter to them?" "Pretty soon, I guess," Heather said. "Well, good luck, Sis!" Scott said, going off to his room.

Heather slowly walked into the kitchen with the last dinner plate and her letter. "Are you feeling all right, tonight?" her mom asked.

Heather's stomach began to flip-flop. "Well, I ... uh ... I have a letter from Ms. Miller," she whispered.

Her mom smiled. "Another Top Citizen Award?" she asked.

Now, Heather felt worse than ever. "No," she sighed, "I think you'd better read it."

It seemed forever until her mother and father finished reading the letter and laid it down in the middle of the table. There was silence. This was the moment Heather had been dreading all day.

"Heather, you must know that your mother and I are very disappointed," her dad said. "We really didn't expect this from you."

"I have a question for you," her mom said, "and I want you to give me an honest answer."

"Okay," Heather said, nervously.

"Ms. Miller wrote that you were the one who called Raymond a name," she said, "but I have a feeling that Sally and Janet were in on this, too. Were they?"

Heather didn't want to lie. She didn't want to tell on her friends either, but her parents were staring at her and waiting for the truth. Reluctantly, she nodded her head.

Mother remarked, "A couple of times I've heard you girls laughing about the way other children look. Some people might call this innocent fun, but I think it's unkind and disrespectful."

"Perhaps you and Janet and Sally have a tendency to egg each other on," her dad said. "You get so wrapped up in your own games that you don't notice how cruel your put-downs are."

"I think you should spend the rest of the evening in your room thinking about a very important question," said Heather's mom.

"What question is that?" Heather asked.

"Think about what you and your friends did to Raymond in class today, and ask yourself, 'What if that were me?'"

Heather thought about this for a moment. "You mean what if that were me wearing braces and being teased?"

"That's right," Dad said, "and your mother and I expect a thoughtful answer from you in the morning before school. Right now it's late so you'd better go to your room and get started."

After Heather got into bed, she thought, "I guess I'd better start thinking if Mom and Dad expect an answer from me in the morning." She pulled the soft warm comforter up around her neck and snuggled down into the cool sheets. "WHAT IF THAT WERE ME?" she wondered, but before she could think of an answer, she fell fast asleep.

"Good morning Ms. Miller," the children giggled.

"Well, you're all in a good mood today," Ms. Miller said, smiling. "What's so funny?"

"That's what's so funny!" Janet and Sally blurted out, pointing at Heather and laughing.

"Why, Heather, you do look different this morning," Ms. Miller remarked.

"Yeah," Janet snickered, "Like something from a different world!"

The whole class roared with laughter.

"I'll bet she's signaling her space ship right now with those antennae she's got on her head," Sally giggled.

Heather didn't have a clue about what was happening.

"Antennae? ... On my head?" She reached up to check her head and was suddenly shocked to find metal wires there. In a panic, she followed the wires down to her mouth and there she discovered a mouth of full metal. She had braces and head gear!

"Yeah," someone shouted, "any minute now her whole ship's likely to beam down and invade our classroom!"

"That's right! And they'll probably make all of us wear those things!" someone laughed.

"Oh, no!" the whole class chanted, "Then we'd all be BRACE FACES!"

Heather was so embarrassed! She prayed the floor would open up and swallow her. How could her friends and classmates be so cruel? Couldn't they see that their jokes and put-downs were hurting her?

"How could they?" she moaned, tossing and turning. Then, suddenly, she awoke with a jolt. Her heart was pounding wildly.

Heather's fingers flew to her mouth. "Oh!" she sighed with relief. "What a terrible nightmare!" Heather was so upset that she scrambled out of bed and rushed down the hall to her parents' bedroom.

"You're okay, honey," her mom whispered. "Everything's all right now."

"Tell us about it?" her dad suggested, patting her back.

Heather explained every detail of the nightmare — especially how badly her friends and classmates had treated her and how terrible the put-downs made her feel.

"Oh, Heather, that was awful!" her mom said. "Especially knowing how much your friends mean to you".

Dad took Heather's hand and said gently, "We can imagine the hurt you felt in your dream when all your friends were calling you names. It must have been terrible. But, you know, this nightmare just might have taught you something."

Heather was silent for a few minutes as she thought. "Now I know how badly Raymond must feel when people put him down because he has braces. It must seem like a nightmare to him every day. I don't understand why his parents make him wear those things."

"Well," her mom said, "what if you woke up one morning, looked in the mirror and discovered a mouthful of crooked, twisted teeth? You couldn't speak clearly or chew food properly, and your friends called you Snaggletooth."

"Oh, no!" Heather groaned, "this sounds like another nightmare."

"But what would you do if it were true?" Dad asked.

"I'd want you to fix my teeth — quick!"

"But that would mean braces for a couple years," Dad explained.

"I know," Heather sighed, "but I think I'd rather be called Brace Face for a couple years than Snaggletooth for the rest of my life!"

"That must be what Raymond's parents thought too," her mom explained.

"They want to make life better for him in the future. I'll bet there's something you could do to make Raymond's life better, too."

"Like apologize?" Heather asked.

"That's a good start," her mom said. "And, who knows, maybe you'll make a new friend."

The next day at school the first thing Heather did was apologize to Raymond. She told him she'd like to be his friend and she invited him to play a game of tether ball before the bell rang. It was a lot of fun!

She didn't talk with Janet or Sally until lunch time when they came running up to ask her what it was like sitting next to FOUR EYES.

"Four Eyes?" Heather asked.

"Yeah, Laura with her new glasses — FOUR EYES!" they snickered.

"It's just as nice sitting next to Laura as it always was — she's a good friend," Heather said. "She's coming to our slumber party Saturday. You'll like her. It'll be nice having someone new join us. I can't wait 'till the party. And, boy," Heather giggled, "do I have a dream to tell you two!

Discussion Questions:

1. Why were Heather and her friends unkind to Raymond?
2. How do you think Raymond felt when Heather and her friends were putting him down? Why didn't the girls consider his feelings?
3. How did Heather feel in her dream? How did the dream change her attitude toward Raymond?
4. What is a put-down? What are some examples of put-downs?
5. Is there any such thing as a "kind" put-down? Explain.
6. What does it mean to be kind?
7. What is the "Golden Rule?"
8. How can we use the Golden Rule to guide our actions toward other people?
9. What are some specific ways that we can show each other kindness here at school?

Four Eyes and Brace Face
Experience Sheet

Think about the story, "Four Eyes and Brace Face." What thoughts do you have about the characters? How did you react to the things they said and did? Use this page to write down anything that comes to mind. Then answer the questions on the next page.

Have you ever been the object of teasing or put-downs? How did you feel and what did you do?

_____

_____

_____

_____

Think of someone you know who is very kind. What are some of the kind things this person does?

_____

_____

_____

Describe an act of kindness that you have done for someone recently:

_____

_____

_____

Think of six kind acts that you can do for friends or family members during the next week. List them here:

_____ _____

_____ _____

_____ _____

A Time I Felt Sorry for Someone Who Was Put Down

A Sharing Circle

Objectives:

The students will:
— express empathy for the feelings of another person.
— describe some of the negative effects of put-downs.
— explain why people use put-downs.
— describe ways of avoiding the habit of putting others down.

Introduce the topic:

Today, we're going to talk about put-downs and how they affect people. Our topic is, "A Time I Felt Sorry for Someone Who Was Put Down." Unfortunately, people seem to put each other down a lot these days. In addition, we see put-downs all the time on television. Many of those put-downs are supposed to come across as clever. This is unfortunate, because put-downs hurt people — even those that are intended as jokes.

Try to remember a time when you observed someone say or do something that made another person feel bad. Maybe the put-down was done as a joke or perhaps it was intended to be hurtful. The incident may have occurred at school, in the neighborhood, at the supermarket or shopping mall, or somewhere else. Without mentioning any names, tell us what happened, how you reacted, and how you think the person who was put down felt. Think it over for a few moments. The topic is, "A Time I Felt Sorry for Someone Who Was Put Down."

Discussion Questions:

1. How did most of us react to seeing another person put down?
2. How do you feel when someone puts you down?
3. Why do people put each other down?
4. How can you prevent yourself from getting in the "put-down" habit?

Something I Did to Make Someone Feel Good

A Sharing Circle

Objectives:

The students will:
— identify specific words and actions that create good feelings in others.
— accept credit for good and kind deeds.
— explain how acts of kindness benefit themselves and others.

Introduce the Topic:

Today's topic is a very broad one that can be discussed in many ways. It is, "Something I Did to Make Someone Feel Good." You see what I mean? You have probably done hundreds of things to make other people feel good. Just tell us about one.

Maybe you gave someone a flower, a present, or a compliment. Perhaps you hugged a friend who was feeling bad, or offered to relieve a parent of a chore or errand. Telling a joke can make someone feel good. So can telling a person what a good job he or she did, or saying, "I like you" or "I love you." Describe what you said or did and how you felt inside. The topic is, "Something I Did to Make Someone Feel Good."

Discussion Questions:

1. How do you feel when you know you've made someone feel good?
2. Usually, when a person feels good, everyone who comes in contact with that person benefits. Can you explain how that happens?
3. If everyone in our class tried to make one extra person feel good each day, how would our class benefit?

A Time I Made Friends With a New Kid

A Sharing Circle

Objectives:
The students will:
— express empathy for other children.
— identify emotions that typically result from being an outsider or newcomer.
— describe ways of assuming responsibility for improving the feelings of another person.

Introduce the Topic:

Those of you who've had the experience of enrolling in a new school where you don't know anyone understand what a lonely, even scary experience it can be. Today we're going to talk about what it's like to reach out to a new person and make the person feel welcome. Our topic is, "A Time I Made Friends With a New Kid."

Although this probably happened at school, it could also have happened in your neighborhood, at church or temple, or in connection with an organization to which you belong, like Little League or scouts. Tell us why you decided to became friends with the new person and how you went about it. Maybe you were seated next to each other and just started talking, or perhaps you realized that the new person was alone much of the time and offered to keep him or her company at recess or walking home after school. Or maybe you became acquainted because you worked on a class project together. Think about it for a few moments. The topic is, "A Time I Made Friends With a New Kid."

Discussion Questions:

1. What was fun for you about making friends with someone new?
2. What did you find difficult about getting to know a new person?
3. Why is reaching out to a new person a kind thing to do?
4. What does it mean to be kind?

A Book of Kindness
Writing and Art Activity

Objectives:
The students will:
— define the term kindness.
— brainstorm examples of kind deeds.
— describe a kind act they did or received.

Materials:
writing materials; drawing paper; colored marking pens, crayons, or pencils; glue; a large three-ring binder

Procedure:

Write the word kindness on the board. Ask the students to help you define its meaning. In the process, make these points about kindness:

- Kindness is a quality that is developed from being kind.

- Being kind means being considerate, thoughtful, or helpful.

- An act of kindness is something you do. It is a deed or behavior. It's possible to have kind thoughts and feelings, but they are private until you express them in an act of kindness.

- A kind act is always done voluntarily, not because it is required.

Ask the students to brainstorm examples of kind acts. List their suggestions on the board. Encourage a variety of ideas, by asking questions like "What are some kind acts you can do for a friend? ...a classmate? ...brother or sister? ...parent? ...neighbor? ...your teacher? ...grandparent? ...a stranger? ...the environment? Include things like:

— make friends with a new student
— offer to share things
— talk to or play with kids who seem left out
— give someone a compliment
— read a story to a younger child
— visit senior citizens in a retirement or rest home
— help a friend do his/her chores
— help a classmate solve a tough math problem
— surprise your parent by doing an "extra" chore at home
— hold a door for someone
— pick up trash when you see it lying around

Announce that the students are going to write about and draw an act of kindness they've done — or one that someone else has done for them. Distribute writing and drawing materials. In your own words, explain:

Describe the kind act, tell who did it, and for whom it was done. You don't have to mention names, just use words like "friend," "teacher," "sister," or "older person." Then write about the feelings of the person who did the kind deed, and the feelings of the person who received it. Draw a picture that shows the kind act being done.

Use whatever system you normally use to have the students correct their spelling and grammar and then complete a rewrite. As a final step, have the students assemble the story and drawing, either by writing a final version somewhere on the drawing itself, or by gluing the drawing to the story page, or vice-versa.

Have the students share their stories and pictures in small groups. Then place all of the finished work in the three-ring binder. Insert a cover page titled, "Book of Kindness." (Have one of the children illustrate the cover page.)

A good way to culminate this activity is by singing the song, *Handle with Care*. sIt can also be read as a poem.

Note:

Adjust the demands of the assignment to the ability levels of your students. Younger students need only write a sentence or two; older ones could be asked to write a true or fictional story about kindness. Have non-writers draw a picture of the kind act and dictate a sentence or two for you or an aide to letter at the bottom of the drawing.

Discussion Questions:

1. Why is it important to try to turn kind thoughts into kind deeds?
2. When you have a kind thought about someone, how can you express it?
3. Why can't chores and assignments ever be acts of kindness?
4. Why do acts of kindness have to be voluntary?

Kindness Makes News

Current Events Research

Objectives:

The students will:
— research current events.
— identify acts of kindness done by other people.
— relate kind actions to civic duty and responsibility.

Materials:

examples of one or two acts of kindness in stories or photos clipped from newspapers; copies of local newspapers, organizational newsletters, and other publications that carry human-interest stories; construction paper; glue; dark-colored marking pens

Note: The research portion of this activity can be given as homework or as a library assignment, with the students assuming responsibility for finding appropriate publications.

Procedure:

Review with the students the definition of an act of kindness:

— considerate, thoughtful or helpful
— an action, not merely a thought
— voluntary

Read the examples of kind acts that you have provided. (Or show them if they are photos.)

Tell the students that you want them to become aware of the kind things that people do for one another, and that one way to do this is to start noticing reports of kind deeds in newspapers, other publications, and from the internet.

Point out that news-reporting organizations, including TV, radio, and newspapers, don't devote very much time or space to reporting "good" news, including good deeds, because such things are not usually considered "news." However, examples of kind acts can be found. For example, a report of hurricane damage might tell about people who have donated blankets and clothing to help the victims. A story about an accident might include a photo of a child being comforted. In addition, most newspapers report on voluntary community activities, like clean-ups, food drives, or other benefits. All of these examples fit the kindness definition.

Tell the students that you want them to search through newspapers, other types of publications, and/or the internet to find examples of kind acts. If you are providing the publications, distribute them. If they are using the internet, the articles will need to be printed or downloaded..

When the students have collected their articles, distribute the construction paper, glue, and markers.

Have the students mount their article on a sheet of construction paper slightly larger than the article itself. Using the marking pen, have them circle or underline the part that describes the deed. Then have them write a new headline for the article that focuses on the act of kindness. For example, if the article was titled, "Hurricane Rosie Batters Florida Coast," the new headline might read, "Thousands Send Aid to Florida."

Have the students get together in groups of four to six and share their articles. Then post the articles on a bulletin board, under the caption "Kindness Makes News!"

Discussion Questions:

1. How did the act of kindness you found out about help the person(s) who received it?
2. Why is it important not to ignore acts of kindness or take them for granted?
3. Why do people help each other in time of need?
4. How do you feel when you do something kind for another person?

The Kindness Link
An Ongoing Recognition Project

Objectives:

The students will:
— purposefully do kind things for one another.
— explain that acts of kindness are self-perpetuating because they promote a spirit of giving and generosity.

Materials:

strips of colored construction paper or other sturdy art paper; marking pens, stapler or tape; box or basket for collecting finished links; a dinner bell or chime

Procedure:

Announce that the class is going to create a "Chain of Kindness" that reaches all around the room. Explain that the chain will be very colorful and attractive and that everyone will have an opportunity to participate in its making. However, the speed with which the chain reaches around the room will depend on how many acts of kindness the students do for each other.

Hold up one of the paper strips. Explain that each link in the chain will be made from a strip just like this one, and show the students where the strips will be kept. (Place the blank strips, markers, and box/basket together, perhaps at an activity center bearing the name Kindness.) Then make the first link as a demonstration. Tell the students about a kind act that you did for someone in the class that day (or describe a kind act that you observed a student do). Then, using a dark marker, write a sentence describing the kind action on the strip. Loop and staple the strip to make a link, with the writing on the outside. Tape the first link to a secure location, such as the frame of a bulletin board.

In your own words explain:

Each of you can make and add links to the chain by doing acts of kindness for members of the class. Remember an act of kindness must be a helpful, considerate or thoughtful <u>action</u>. It must also be voluntary — something you do because you want to, not because you have to. When you do a kind act, get a strip of paper and write a sentence on it describing what you did. You may also make a strip for someone who is kind to you as long as that person doesn't make one, too. Only one strip per kind action. Put your finished strip in the box/basket. Once a day, we'll read all the links. If your description fits the definition of an act of kindness, you'll get to attach your link to the chain. There is no limit to the number of links you can add — as long as each one is for a different act of kindness.

Once a day, read aloud the completed strips from the box/basket. After a strip is read, allow the student who did the kindness to attach and staple the strip to the end of the chain, making a new link. If you have a bell or chime, ring it while you announce the addition of a new link to the kindness chain.

Discussion Questions:

1. When someone is kind to you, are you more likely or less likely to be kind to others? Why?
2. Is kindness "catching?" How is it spread?
3. How do you feel when someone does something kind for you?
4. What are some examples of very small acts of kindness? What are some examples of very big acts of kindness?

Kindness Coupons
A Writing and Design Project

Objectives:
The students will:
— identify kind acts that can be done for different people.
— commit to future acts of kindness by describing them in writing.

Materials:
samples of coupons or coupon books; 8 1/2-inch by 11-inch sheets of sturdy white paper cut horizontally into three equal pieces (8 1/2 by 3 2/3); several sheets of colored construction paper cut to the same size or slightly larger; colored markers, pencils or crayons; decorative stickers (optional); stapler

Procedure:
On the board, write the headings **Parents, Friend, Brother/Sister, Grandparents**. Ask the students to help you list acts of kindness that they could do for each of these people. For example:

Parents

wash dishes
give a massage
give a big hug
watch the baby
give a compliment
carry the groceries
clean and sort a drawer or shelf

When you have generated several items under each heading, announce that the students are each going to make a Kindness Coupon Book to give to their parents or to some other person. Each page will have a coupon that can be torn out and redeemed for a specific act of kindness. A description of the kind action will be written on the page. The students can decorate the coupons with borders, fancy lettering, symbols, drawings, or stickers (if available).

Give each student six to ten sheets of cut paper and two pieces of colored construction paper. Immediately, have the students make a sharp crease in each white sheet about 1–1/2 inches from the left edge. Tell them not to draw or write on the left section because this is where the coupons will be stapled together. The crease will allow for easy tearing.

Make two coupons yourself to demonstrate the process. Draw a border. Inside the border, write or print a description of the kind action and any instructions for receiving it. For example, "5-Minute Back Massage — Good any evening 6:00 - 8:00 p.m." Decorate with a drawing of a hand or some other symbol. Make a second sample. Then place the coupons between two pieces of colored construction paper to create front and back covers. Staple the left edge securely. On the front cover, print "Kindness Coupon Book" in large dark letters.

Make the art materials available. Circulate to make sure that students who do not want to make a book for parents have chosen another recipient, e.g., a grandparent or friend. Encourage the students to collaborate.

Allow time for the students to circulate and informally share their finished books.

Discussion Questions:

1. Why do acts of kindness — even very small ones — make parents happy?
2. Do you sometimes need permission before doing something for a person? When?
3. What could you say or do if your parent turned in a coupon when you didn't feel like doing the kind act?

Variation:

You may prefer to have older students make a coupon book to carry with them, rather than give to someone else. The coupons are torn out by the student and given to different people, then redeemed by those people for specific acts of kindness. This method allows the student to control the process, which ensures that the kind acts are always voluntary.

Kindly Correspondence
Letter Writing and Discussion

Objectives:
The students will:
— identify a person who is important to them.
— describe their feelings about that person both verbally and in writing.

Materials:
one or two sheets of "stationary" for each student (duplicated from computer-generated masters as described under "Procedure"); envelopes; writing implements; stamps (optional)

Procedure:

Use a computer and page-layout program to design two or three different stationary templates. Depending on the ages, needs, and preferences of your students, incorporate some or all of the following:
- borders, fancy or plain
- decorative letters, symbols, or images
- a quotation about kindness, such as the Golden Rule
- a heading, such as "I Appreciate You!" or "You Mean a Lot to Me!"
- sentence starters to mark the salutation, body, closing and signature. For example:

Dear...
You mean a lot to me because...
Sincerely,

Make enough copies of each master to give your students a choice of "stationary" design.

Write the following topic on the board: *Someone Who Means a Lot to Me*

Ask the students to close their eyes and picture someone who means a lot to them. In your own words, say:

Think of some of the reasons that this person is important to you. What does the person do that you appreciate? What do you count on the person for? What do you especially like about the person?

After the students have had a few moments to think individually and quietly, ask them to form dyads or triads and share their thoughts.

Announce that the students are going to have an opportunity to do something kind for the person they shared about. They are going to write a letter to that person, stating why the person means so much to them. Engage the students in a brief discussion, helping them to see how their shared thoughts can be captured in writing.

Distribute envelopes and writing implements and set out stacks of stationary. Suggest that the students write their letter first on scratch paper, correct and rewrite, and then copy the letter to a sheet of stationary.

Students who are going to hand deliver their letters need only write a name or title (e.g. "Mom" "Grampa") on the envelope. Those who must mail their letters may require either your help or that of parents to obtain correct addresses and stamps. In the latter case, a brief note to parents should suffice.

Discussion Questions:

1. How would you feel if you received a letter similar to the one you wrote? How do you think the person you wrote to will feel?
2. Why is it important to let people know how much they mean to us?
3. What are some other ways that you can express your appreciation for people you care about?

Variations:

Have a team of students design and produce several types of stationary. Or, if time and equipment permit, have every student design his/her own stationary.

HANDLE WITH CARE

CHORUS

Where there is hatred, I'll bring love;
We can settle things by talking, you'll see.
Where there is sadness, I'll bring joy;
I'll help you to smile again.
Where there's been harm done, I'll ease the pain,
And help the forgiving begin.

(1)
My vision is all people living in peace,
Though I can't change the world in a day,
I'll start with myself and the people I know,
And from there the caring will grow.
To help stop the hating and hurting and fear,
Here is what I'm going to do . . .

CHORUS

(2)
Instead of waiting for you to dry my tears,
I'll dry yours, and comfort you.
Instead of waiting for you to understand me,
I'll do my best to understand you.
Instead of waiting for you to love me,
I'll show my love for you.

CHORUS

(3)
I rejoice when you feel glad.
I'm concerned when you feel sad.
I'll do my best to care for you,
And welcome your caring for me; for treating
Others with care and respect for their rights
Is the only way we'll live in peace.

CHORUS

Music is available, as a download, from www.songsforteaching.com

Copyright 1996 by Linda K. Williams

Tolerance

Story:

Randy Learns About Tolerance
Experience Sheet

Sharing Circles:

Something I Respect About a Person of a Different Race or Culture
A Friend I Have Who Is Different From Me

Activities:

The Roots of Tolerance
Researching and Reporting Family Histories

Hand to Hand
Simulating Stereotypes

Meet Pebble Pete
Recognizing Unique Characteristics

If the Shoe Fits
An Experiment in Categorizing

Behind the Labels, We're All People
Discussion and Song

Song:

Another Word for People

Randy Learns About Tolerance

by Dianne Schilling

Tolerance. The word was everywhere. In big plastic letters on the sign outside the main office, just below where it said Kennedy Elementary School. Lettered across the top of bulletin boards in all the classrooms. Imbedded in colorful posters hung throughout the halls. On the inside curved walls of the school buses. Tolerance — the word of the month.

Well, it was more than a word. Tolerance was the *moral value* of the month. Last month the moral value was Caring and the month before it was Respect. In January, the first month to have a value, all the signs said Honesty.

On Monday, Ms. Bartels told her 5th-grade class to look up the meaning of the word. "After you've done your research, be thinking about what tolerance means to you," she said. "Next week, I'll ask you to share some of your ideas."

"It's hard *not* to think about it," eleven-year-old Randy sighed to himself. "Tolerance is everywhere you look."

That evening, as Randy and his dad, Henry, were clearing away the dinner dishes, Henry looked at his wife and asked, "Why are you so tired tonight, Corinne?"

"Phil was out sick again today. The office was super busy and I had to do his work plus my own," answered Randy's mom, wearily scooping spilled applesauce from the front of Jesse's coveralls. Jesse was Randy's baby brother.

"You're too *tolerant*, Corinne. Phil misses work all the time. He takes advantage of you. If you weren't so willing to cover for him, he'd have been fired long ago," Randy's dad said.

"But what if he really is sick, Henry? The least I can do is help."

"What does tolerant mean?" Randy interrupted.

"What?" Randy's mother looked startled, like she'd forgotten Randy was there.

"Dad said you're too tolerant," Randy repeated. "What's 'tolerant'?"

"It means your mother puts up with too much guff from Phil," said Henry firmly. "She should put her foot down."

"Now Henry, I know you're thinking of me, but you don't understand what it's like at my office," Corinne argued.

Randy was puzzled by his father's reply, but he decided not to interrupt again.

"You're feeding the baby table foods Corinne? Isn't it too soon?" asked Aunt Rita, who stopped by every Tuesday with ideas and advice for everyone.

"Jess seems to *tolerate* them just fine, Aunt Rita. Don't worry, I'm not giving him meat or olives or anything. Just soft things." Intently, Jesse worked several slippery strands of spaghetti into his mouth.

"Mom, he really *likes* the spaghetti," said Randy.

"Yes, Randy. That's what I was telling Aunt Rita."

"No...., you said Jess *tolerates* it. That means he puts up with it. But I think he likes it," insisted Randy.

"I meant his *system* tolerates solid food, Randy. You know — his stomach. Sometimes babies can't eat what everybody else eats. But Jesse's system tolerates it." explained Corrine.

"What would happen if his system didn't tolerate it, Mom?" asked Randy.

"He'd spit it up," Aunt Rita declared. "So be careful — tolerance has its limits!"

Randy made a face. That was a strange kind of tolerance.

"Have you seen the new boy who moved in on the corner?" Randy asked his mother. "He looks funny."

"Yes, I've seen him from a distance," answered Corrine. "He has come from Africa to live with the Stewarts. He may look a little different from most of the folks we know, Randy. Maybe he even does some things a little differently. But inside I'm sure he's a lot like you."

"He'll probably go to my school. He's in for trouble if he does," Randy thought out loud.

"What do you mean?" demanded Corrine. "Why would there be trouble?"

"Because he's different, Mom. If you don't fit in, you get teased. Kids say things."

Randy's mother snorted angrily and slammed her open palm on the kitchen counter. "Something is seriously wrong if we can't have a little *tolerance* for each other's differences," she said. "I expect you to be nice to that new boy, Randy."

"Do you mean I should put up with him?" asked Randy, "Or do you mean he shouldn't make my stomach sick?" Randy was experimenting with the word, but his mother didn't think it was funny.

"Tolerance means accepting other people," said Corrine sternly. "Everybody can't be just like us."

Sure enough, the new boy from the Stewart house was at school the very next day. And he was in Randy's class.

"Students, this is Josephat Nmbura. Josephat is from Tanzania, which is a country in Africa," said Ms. Bartels, gesturing toward the thin, dark boy seated near the front of the room.

The new boy jumped to his feet and smiled broadly, revealing a gap in his lower front teeth. "I am being happy to know American school," he said, his words thickly accented. Several children laughed.

"Josephat is learning English," smiled Ms. Bartels, "so be sure to help him. Ernesto, would you like to find Tanzania on the map and show the rest of us where it is?"

While Ernesto studied the big world map on the wall, two dozen pairs of eyes studied Josephat. Randy tried to figure out what was different about him. At least half the class was African-American, so it wasn't his skin color. Maybe it was the way he sat so straight, and the way he kept smiling. His clothing was like the other boys, but his hair was shaved close to his head. Then Randy saw the circles. A small round mark, like the imprint from a bottle cap, high on each cheek. Randy wondered why a kid would paint circles on his face.

During lunch recess, Randy and two friends checked out a soccer ball and practiced kicks and fancy footwork on the grass. Their breathless attempts to outdo each other were interrupted by loud laughter coming from the lunch tables a few yards away. Curious, they stopped their game and moved in that direction.

Several students were gathered around Josephat. Some were laughing and pointing. Others were huddled together whispering and giggling. Josephat, smiling as always, looked confused. The empty space between his teeth made him look a little dumb, too, Randy thought.

Gary, a big sixth-grader who was always acting smart, said to the group, "He gave me most of his lunch! Half the sandwich, the apple, most of the cookies. Every time he pulled something out of the bag, he handed it to me. Then he acted like I was supposed to give him my lunch. I guess he thought we were having a picnic!" Gary doubled over laughing.

Randy thought about tolerance. He remembered little Jess and Aunt Rita, and wondered if it was his turn to be sick. Instead, he took a deep breath and yelled to Gary and anyone else who was listening, "Leave Josephat alone. So what if he thought it was a picnic? Maybe they have picnics in Africa."

Seconds later, the bell rang. The students quickly forgot about Josephat and headed for their classrooms. Randy walked silently beside Josephat. Out of the corner of his eye, he studied the circle on Josephat's left cheek. It wasn't painted on; it was part of Josephat's skin. "A scar," Randy thought.

All afternoon, and for the next two days, Josephat kept the kids in Randy's class amused. Every time Ms. Bartels called on him or even mentioned his name, Josephat jumped to his feet, grinning. Twice Randy laughed with the other kids and then felt guilty. The first time Ms. Bartels asked Josephat to help pass out some papers, he answered very seriously, "Yes, Mama." All the kids looked at each other in disbelief, then burst out laughing. For the rest of the day, Ms. Bartels was "Mama" to some of the class clowns. "Yes Mama" this, and "Yes Mama" that.

Josephat's English was slow and oddly phrased. Randy could see smirks and hear giggles every time Josephat spoke. Two boys in the back of the room made a game of imitating Josephat's stiff posture.

All the while *Tolerance* in big black bulletin-board letters loomed over the class. Like the giant oak tree in front of the school, *Tolerance* was part of the scenery — so nobody saw it.

On Saturday morning, Bob came over from next door to help Henry with the room addition. The breakfast nook was becoming a family room and part of the back yard was being lost in the process.

"What's the *tolerance* of that window opening, Henry?" Bob asked.

"Oh, about a half-inch, I think."

"*Tolerance*, Dad? Are you sure Bob meant *tolerance*?" asked Randy.

"Sure, son. Tolerance is how much leeway we have in choosing a window to fit the opening. The measurements have to be close, but they don't have to be exact. We can tighten up the fit when we add the frame around the window."

Randy picked up a measuring tape from the floor and checked the size of the window opening. He pushed the button on the metal case and watched the tape shoot back inside. He was surprised that *tolerance* could be measured.

Randy wandered into the living room, used his foot to push Jess's abandoned toys out of the way, and sprawled on the nubby beige carpet. He decided to watch a video. Rummaging through stacks of tapes, Randy found one of his favorites and, in seconds, tolerance was far from his mind — but not for long. Twenty minutes into *Raiders of the Lost Ark*, Randy's mother huffed through the doorway and shouted above the noise, "Randy, I will not *tolerate* the condition of your room a moment longer! Get in there and do something about it, and no more TV until it's clean!"

Randy groaned and flicked off the DVD. "Will tolerate, won't tolerate, too tolerant, not tolerant enough," he thought. "I think *everybody's* confused about tolerance."

────────────────

On Sunday afternoon, Duane and Michael came over. They played computer games and rode their bikes to the park where they sat on the grass and talked about summer vacation.

"If you could do anything you wanted this summer, what would you choose?" asked Randy.

Duane thought a minute. "I'd go on one of those cruises," he said. "My cousin went on a Caribbean cruise and ended up with three days at Disney World. That'd be cool."

"What about you, Michael?" asked Randy.

"I'd go visit my grandfather in Idaho and go fishing," answered Michael. "Gramps knows all the best rivers and camping spots."

"If I could do anything," said Randy, "I'd work at the zoo this summer. Sometimes they let kids have jobs as keeper's aides."

"That's a stupid idea," said Duane. "If you could do anything you wanted, why stay here? You're here all year long. Go to Hawaii or Paris or China."

"It's not a stupid idea," said Randy. "I want to learn about animals."

"But that's like school," said Michael. "You probably get graded and everything. Duane's right. Do something fun, not something nerdy."

"Randy's always a nerd," said Duane. "He doesn't know what fun is."

"Oh yeah, why'd you come over today then?" asked Randy. "If I'm so boring, why come to my house at all?"

"Because I couldn't think of anything better to do, that's why," said Duane. "Com'on Mike, let's go. I don't want to keep 'Randa-the-Panda' from dreaming about the zoo."

────────────────

As Randy rode his bike home, he thought about what his friends had said. He really *did* want to work at the zoo. He had a right to his own idea of fun. Duane and Michael were just being selfish. They were being . . .

"Intolerant," Randy said out loud. The word popped out from some corner of his brain, surprising him and causing him to swerve sharply. He had just rounded the corner in front of the Stewart's house, and a friendly voice called out, "Hey, slow down Randy! It's not even dinnertime!"

It was Mr. Stewart working inside his open garage. Randy was embarrassed. He must have been riding faster than he realized. He pulled his bike around and stopped. Getting off, he let the bike drop gently on the front lawn. "Sorry, Mr. Stewart," Randy said, walking into the garage.

"You must have been thinking hard about something," laughed Mr. Stewart. "You've met Josephat, haven't you?"

It was then that Randy saw Josephat, sitting on a stool near the back of the garage. Josephat smiled and stood up. Randy said hello. He couldn't think of anything else to say, and the two boys just stood there looking at each other self-consciously.

After a moment, Mr. Stewart looked around from his workbench. "Josephat, why don't you take Randy inside and get him a glass of water."

"Oh, no thanks," said Randy quickly. "I'd better be getting home."

"What's the hurry?" asked Mr. Stewart. "Like I said, it's not even dinnertime. And besides, Josephat needs the practice." Mr. Stewart winked at Randy, making it impossible for him to leave.

Josephat poured two glasses of water and gave one to Randy, who drank it thirstily. "Thanks," Randy said, setting the empty glass on the counter. He looked at Josephat and felt stupidly speechless. Finally, he asked, "Want to show me your room?"

"My room?" repeated Josephat. "Oh, yes. Come."

Josephat's small room had what looked to Randy like African pictures on the walls, along with framed photographs of people in large and small groups. Josephat explained that these were school friends in Tanzania. Carved animals sat in groups on the dresser, bookcase, and bedside table. "Wow," said Randy, picking up a painted wood giraffe.

"You like the giraffe? Please, you must have it," said Josephat.

"No, no," Randy said politely. "It's yours. Randy's finger traced the smooth surface of a carved elephant.

"Then take elephant," insisted Josephat.

Every time Randy saw something he liked, Josephat tried to give it to him. Randy stopped admiring Josephat's things, and instead looked at Josephat. His eyes went to the circles on Josephat's cheeks.

"All boys have," explained Josephat. "In Maasai tribe, a sign of beauty," he said. He pointed to his cheeks and said, "Only boys." Then he pointed to the gap where his lower front tooth had been cut out, saying, "Girls, too." Josephat laughed and said, "I must get a tooth for America. Not beautiful here."

Josephat and Randy both laughed.

On Monday morning, Ms. Bartels pointed to the word *Tolerance* on the bulletin board. She asked the students to reflect on what they learned about tolerance during the past week. She told them to write at least five sentences about tolerance, and then she asked volunteers to read what they had written. Randy raised his hand. When Ms. Bartels called on him, he read:

Tolerance is putting up with something you don't like.

Tolerance is being able to eat something without getting sick.

Tolerance is when a window or door doesn't have to fit exactly.

Tolerance is when it's okay for your friend to spend his summer doing something that he thinks is fun — even if you don't think it's fun.

Tolerance is accepting when a person looks different or has different ideas or different ways of doing things.

When the noon bell rang, Randy took his lunch and went outside. He found Josephat sitting at a lunch table and scooted in next to him. Randy opened his lunch. He took out a sandwich, grapes, carrot sticks, and cookies. He spread everything out on the table. Josephat did the same.

Then Randy gave half of everything he had to Josephat who, laughing, did the same in return.

When other kids walked by, Randy said, "Josephat and I are having a picnic. Want to join us? Several children did.

Discussion Questions:

1. What were the different definitions of tolerance that Randy discovered?
2. Why did the other children make fun of Josephat?
3. How was Josephat different from the other children? How was he the same?
4. How do you think Josephat felt as a new student in a strange country?
5. What does it mean to recognize the beliefs and practices of another person?
6. Does recognizing and accepting a person's beliefs and practices mean that you have to agree with them or make them your own? Explain.

Randy Learns About Tolerance
Experience Sheet

Randy's teacher told the students to think about what tolerance meant to them. Here's a place to write about what tolerance means to *you*:

_____
_____
_____
_____
_____
_____
_____
_____

Has anyone ever been intolerant of you or something about you? What happened and how did you feel?

_____
_____
_____
_____
_____
_____
_____
_____
_____
_____

Something I Respect About a Person of a Different Race or Culture

A Sharing Circle

Objectives:

The students will:
—identify the basis for their respect for someone of a different race or culture.
—demonstrate tolerance for people with different beliefs and practices.

Introduce the Topic:

Our topic today is, "Something I Respect About a Person of a Different Race or Culture." This is a topic that will probably take a little thought. The person you choose to talk about can be someone you know personally or someone you don't know but have heard about. The important thing is that you have a feeling of respect for this person. I'd like you to explore the reasons behind that respect.

For example, maybe you have a neighbor who is of a different race and you respect him because he is friendly and helpful to everyone who lives on your street. Or perhaps someone in your family married a person from a different culture and you respect her because she is very smart, or very funny, or very understanding. Maybe you've heard or read about the leader of another nation, and you respect that person's ideas about how to have peace in the world. Or maybe you know about the head of an organization or cultural group and you think that person is a great leader. Remember that respect can be earned in small ways, too. Maybe you respect this person for something as simple as smiling, being honest, accepting others, or showing pride in his or her culture. Take a few moments to consider the topic. It is, "Something I Respect About a Person of a Different Race or Culture."

Discussion Questions:

1. Why do people have such different ideas? Why do they do things so differently?
2. What can you learn from people who have different beliefs and customs than you have?
3. What is tolerance?
4. How can you become a more tolerant person?

A Friend I Have Who Is Different From Me

A Sharing Circle

Objectives:

The students will:
— demonstrate that friendships form across racial, cultural, and other types of boundaries.
— describe the relative importance of commonalties and differences in a friendship.

Introduce the Topic:

Today we're going to talk about our friends, particularly the ones who are different from us in some significant way. Our topic is, "A Friend I Have Who Is Different From Me."

Tell us about a friend of yours who is either much older or much younger, is of a different race or culture, or is very different from you in some other way. Tell us how you became friends with this person and what you like about him or her. I'll give you a few moments to decide what you want to share. Our topic is, "A Friend I Have Who Is Different From Me."

Discussion Questions:

1. What were the reasons we gave for liking these friends and valuing their friendship?
2. What, if any, problems or conflicts have been caused by the difference between you and your friend, and how have you handled them?
3. What have you and your friend been able to learn from each other as a result of your differences?
4. What is more important between friends, the things you have in common or your differences? Why?

The Roots of Tolerance
Researching and Reporting Family Histories

Objectives:
The students will:
— identify their countries of origin.
— interview family members to learn about ancestral experiences.
— explain that all families were once immigrants to the U.S.
— experience the diversity that exists among their classmates.

Materials:
writing materials for the students; U.S. and world maps; colored pins, flags or other map markers; whiteboard

Procedure:

Introduce this activity by explaining that the United States is a land of many different people, all of whom have the right to share in its benefits and freedoms. Point out that no one ethnic group "owns" the U.S. because all of its citizens, or their ancestors, came from some other land.

Announce that the students are going to do some individual research to find out what lands they, their parents, grandparents, or earlier ancestors came from. They will also learn some interesting things about the perceptions and experiences of these members of their family.

Have the students ask their parents and/or grandparents where they were born. Ask them to find out how and why their parents and/or grandparents came to the U.S. from another country, or to your part of the country from another region. Generate a list of questions for the students to answer by talking with family members or searching family records. (If you are working with very young children, send a note home explaining the activity and listing appropriate questions for the parents to answer.) Examples are:

- What kind of work did family members do in their country of origin?
- Where did they go to school and what was school like?
- Why did they come to the United States?
- In which U.S. states and communities have they lived?
- What was it like to leave home and go where they didn't know anyone or what to expect?
- What things were the same in both countries/regions and what things were different?
- What are some problems they encountered when they moved to the U.S.?
- Did family members experience any discrimination when they came to the U.S.? How have they handled it?

Have the students report orally to the class. Schedule two or three reports each day and allow plenty of time for reactions and discussion. On U.S. and world maps, using colored pins or flags, mark the various places the students and their families/ancestors have lived. (For example, use one color to show countries of ancestral origin and a different color to mark places where the students have lived.) Help the students to gain an awareness of distances involved. Talk about various modes of transportation used and the different types of schools attended by children.

Create a classroom chart listing every student along with his/her country or state of origin and ancestral countries of origin. Have the students locate a picture of the flag of each country represented and replicate it with colored markers on art paper or by making a collage of the flag with colored construction paper. Use the flag art to decorate the chart.

Finally, invite some of the parents/grandparents to visit the class and share their experiences personally.

Discussion Questions:

1. How many different countries are represented in our class?
2. Which countries that you've heard about particularly interest you?
3. How can we all benefit from the various cultures and histories represented in our class?
4. What is tolerance and what have you learned about tolerance from this activity?

Hand to Hand

Simulating Stereotypes

Objectives:
The students will:
— describe what it is like to be discriminated against because of a superficial characteristic.
— identify groups that are frequently stereotyped in this country.
— define the terms *prejudice, stereotype, and discrimination.*

Materials:
non-permanent marking pens in two colors; whiteboard; writing materials for the students

Procedure:

As students enter the room, mark their left palm with either an X or an O. Don't offer any explanation for this procedure. However, do instruct the students at the beginning of class to show the marked palm whenever they raise their hands to ask a question.

Write the following words on the chalkboard:
prejudice
stereotype
discrimination

Ask the students to help you define the meaning of each word. However, as the students raise their hands to suggest ideas, call on only the X's. Facilitate the discussion and the formulation of each definition just as you would normally, while ignoring the O's and lavishing praise and positive reinforcement on the X's. Say things like:

> *That's an excellent insight, Mike.*
> *Yes, yes, Monica, you are absolutely correct.*
> *You X's are really sharp today.*

Within a very short time, the O's will stop raising their hands, become distracted, and find other things to occupy their attention. Some will realize what you are doing, but others will not. As soon as you have "lost" almost all of the O's, finish defining whatever word you are on and then stop. Ask the students:

> *What's been happening here?*

Invite the students to give their reactions to your process. When accused of favoring the X's, admit it. Tell the students

that you wanted them to experience prejudice, stereotyping and discrimination first hand. Ask the students:
—*How did you feel when I wouldn't call on you?*
—*What was it like to hear the X's getting all that praise and attention when you knew that your ideas were just as good?*

Then proceed to the next stage of the experiment. Have every X pair up with an O. In your own words, say to the students:

Actually, I knew all along that the O's were the smartest group and would have the best ideas. I just wanted to give the X's a head start because I knew they needed it. But since the X's didn't get very far, it's time they got some help from the O's. Your assignment is to work with your partner to define the rest of the words. Use the dictionary if you like, and write down your own ideas. O's, you will have to take the lead, because the X's need some help. X's, pay attention to the O's.

Have the pairs proceed with the assignment. Allow this part of the experiment to continue for several minutes. You will probably notice that the O's, rather than show empathy based on their earlier experience, will take great pleasure in dominating the X's. When you think the X's have had ample time to experience their share of discrimination, stop the activity and facilitate a final discussion.

In the course of the discussion, finish defining the terms. Ask the partners to share ideas they generated while working together (if any emerged). Record suggestions and definitions on the board.

Discussion Questions:

1. How did you feel when I implied that you were not very smart?
2. On what basis was I discriminating against each group?
3. Were there any good reasons for me to favor the X's? ...the O's?
4. What groups in our country have been, or are, stereotyped based on something superficial like an X or an O?
5. What if this were not just a short lesson? How would you feel if you were treated every day like you were slower or less able to succeed? How would you act? How well would you do in school?

Important Note:

Although this powerful activity was originally conducted over 40 years ago using eye color, and it has been repeated in thousands of classrooms since then, the nature of the activity could potentially upset some sensitive children. You, as the teaching or counseling professional, should be familiar with the activity beforehand and determine how far to take it. The internet provides a wealth of background information and instruction, and we recommend that you do some research prior to implementation. Use a search engine to find the brown eye, blue eye experiment.

Meet Pebble Pete

An Experiment in the Recognition of Unique Characteristics

Objectives:

The students will:
— describe the unique characteristics of one member of a group of similar objects.
— compare the stereotyping of objects to the stereotyping of people.
— explain that it is the responsibility of the viewer to differentiate one person from another.

Materials:

a paper bag containing a collection of small rocks or pebbles, all very similar in size, shape, and color (apples, oranges, potatoes, or nuts may be substituted)

Procedure:

Begin by asking the students: *Have you ever noticed how people tend to generalize about other people? By "generalize," I mean lump people together in groups. We usually only do that with people we don't know very well. It's hard to stereotype a friend.*

Have the students sit in a large circle. Open the paper bag and show the pebbles to the students. In your own words, say:

These pebbles all look pretty much the same at first glance. But that's because you don't know them. Therefore, I'm going to give you an opportunity to meet and become acquainted with one of these pebbles.

Pass around the bag full of pebbles and have each student reach in and take one. When the bag returns to you, choose a pebble for yourself. Direct the students to take 1 minute to examine their pebble very carefully — to notice its features and everything unique about it so they can introduce it to the group. After 1 minute, begin the sharing by introducing your own pebble. For example, say something like:

I'd like you to meet Pebble Pete. Pete began his life on a mountainside in New Mexico. When he was first chipped from his mother, who was a big boulder, he hit the ground and kept sliding — right down the mountain! That experience scratched him up quite a bit. During his first winter, he was washed into a river and spent almost four years traveling downstream. The water smoothed him out, but I can still see one or two scratches on this side. Finally Pete came ashore near the wide mouth of the river and was eventually scooped up by a man who collected pebbles in his pickup truck and sold them to the landscapers and nurseries in town. That's how I met Pebble Pete. Now he has a job on a pathway in my garden.

Go around the circle and invite the students to introduce their pebbles to the group. When the last pebble has been introduced, thank the students. Then pass the empty bag around, instructing the students to return their pebble to the collection. (Be sure you remove any extra pebbles from the bag before you recollect.)

Ask the students: *Now that you and your pebble have become friends, do you think that it will still look just like all the other pebbles? Let's find out. I'm going to put all the pebbles in the center of the circle so that you can find yours and take it back. The last pebble on the floor should be Pebble Pete.*

Roll the pebbles out of the bag onto the floor. Allow two or three students at a time to examine the pebbles, identify the one they had, and take their pebble "friend" back to their seat. (If someone takes Pete by mistake, express your concern and check the children's pebbles to find him and trade.) Conclude the activity with a discussion.

Discussion Questions:

1. Have you ever heard someone say, "They're all alike"? What will you think the next time you hear that expression?
2. Why do people lump others into groups and pretend they are all alike?
3. What can you say or do if you hear someone stereotyping a person based on color, sex, religion, or some other characteristic?
4. Whose job is it to see and acknowledge the differences between one person and another?

Extension:

Allow the students to decorate their pebbles with miniature designs. Have them apply opaque paints with the tips of small brushes or with Q-tips.

If the Shoe Fits

An Experiment in Categorizing

Objectives:

The students will:
— categorize objects according to a variety of criteria.
— explain that a category both includes and excludes members.
— list categories into which we routinely group people.
— discuss the benefits and drawbacks of categorizing people.

Materials:

a variety of single shoes — old, new, dress, casual, sandals, sneakers, child's, adult's, representing a variety of colors, sizes, styles and heel heights (the more samples, the better); instead of real shoes, you could provide pictures of shoes from catalogs and advertisements

Procedure:

Have the students sit in a circle. Spread the shoes out on the floor in the center of the circle.

Ask the students to look at the shoes and come up with suitable categories for grouping the shoes. (In addition to the categories mentioned under "Materials," you might have shoes that are athletic, hiking, formal, orthopedic, rain, snow, etc.)

Next, see if you can pair the categories. For example:

child	adult
dress	casual
old	new
leather	fabric
high heel	low heel
open	closed

Taking one set of categories at a time, have the students physically arrange the shoes into the two groups. Ask the students to notice:
— Which shoes don't seem to fit either category and are therefore "left out" after each grouping.
— which shoes fit the most categories and which the fewest.
— Which categories are more inclusive and which are less.
— Which categories seem better than others and why.
— How they decide where to put a shoe when it fits two categories equally.
— if they try to bend or stretch a category so that a shoe fits.

Talk about the purpose of having categories and groups. Who is helped by grouping and labeling shoes? Point out that whenever a category is created to include certain items, it automatically excludes others. In a culminating discussion, turn the attention of students from shoes to people, and examine how these concepts and insights apply to the categorizing of people, too. Brainstorm and list all the different people categories that the students can think of. Refer to the list throughout the discussion.

Discussion Questions:

1. How do we categorize people?
2. Who is helped by categorizing people?
2. What groups of people have not been accepted by the dominant culture during our history? How were they treated?
3. How do you feel when you are excluded (left out)?
4. How do groups of people feel when the culture excludes or limits them? What do they do?

Behind the Labels, We're All People

Discussion and Song

Objectives:
The students will:
—identify ethnic and racial groupings and labels.
—discuss the differences between various labels used to describe the same group.
—describe positive and negative outcomes produced by the use of labels.

Materials:
one copy of the song, "Another Word for People" for each student; a pre-selected or arranged melody for the song; whiteboard

Procedure:
Announce that in this activity, the students are going to examine some of the labels and categories used to define groups of people.

Ask the students:
—*How do the terms we use to identify various racial and ethnic groups affect our identity?*
—*Which labels are preferred and why?*

List some of the categories and labels on the board. For example:

- Indian, American Indian, Native American, Tribal Affiliation (Navajo)
- Black, African-American
- Hispanic, Chicano, Mexican, Mexican-American, Latino, or...
- Asian, Oriental, Japanese-American, Chinese-American, Southeast Asian

If you have Hispanic students in the class, ask if they can explain the differences between the various Hispanic labels. Ask which they prefer. Do the same with African-American and Asian-American students, and any other groups that are represented in the class.

Talk about the purpose of ethnic, racial, and nationalistic labels. Use the discussion questions below and encourage the students to generate their own questions. Conclude the activity with the song, Another Word for People."

Distribute the song sheets and explain how the words are "zippered in." Play or sing the melody you have selected or arranged. Then teach it to the students. Refer to the "Performance Suggestions" (at the bottom of the song sheet) for more ideas.

Discussion Questions:

1. Why do we use ethnic labels when we're all just people?
2. What positive things result from emphasizing our ethnic and racial backgrounds? What negative things result?
3. Which do people have more of, similarities or differences? Explain.
4. What would it be like in our country if no one used ethnic or racial labels, or even noticed those kinds of differences? Do you think we'll ever get to that place?

Another Word for "People"

The following song is known as a "zipper" song. The short verse is repeated numerous times, using pairs of nouns inserted in the two blanks. The nouns — names of different groups or categories of people — can be decided in advance, or can be spontaneously suggested by the singers.

*_____ *is just another word for PEOPLE,*
**_____ *is just another word for PEOPLE;*
We're much more alike than the labels make it seem,
And we all call this earth our home.

(Add after the last verse:)
Yes, we all call this earth our home.

1. **Americans** *
   Iraqis ** (or any other nationalities)

2. **Christians** *
   Muslims ** (or any other religions groups

3. **Blacks** *
   Whites **

4. **Disabled** *
   Retarded ** (or any other group similarly subject to stereotyping)

5. **Immigrants** *
   Homeless ** (or any other groups that are heard/read about often and are likely to be part of the "faceless masses" in many minds)

6. **Doctors** *
   Waiters ** (or any other professions)

7. **Parents** *
   Children ** (or choose any two age groups/family role groups)

8. **Enemies** *
   Yes, enemies **

Performance Suggestions:
- Use the "call and response" method to zipper in each new word.
- Give each singer a large card with one of the nouns printed on it. Have the singers hold the card over their face during their "zippered" verse, until the word "people" is sung. — then remove the card revealing the singer's face.

Music is available, as a download, from www.songsforteaching.com

Copyright 1996 by Linda K. Williams

Respect

Story:

How the Turkey Became a Star
Experience Sheet

Sharing Circles:

Something About Me That's Likable and Worthy of Respect
How I Show Respect Toward Others

Activities:

On the Other Hand
Interviews, Drawing and Discussion

The Respectful Classroom
Developing a Classroom Compact

Dear Advice Person
Writing and Discussion

A Big Book of Respect
A Writing and Art Project

A Web of Respect
Game, Discussion and Poetry Reading

Song/Poem:

No One Is a Nobody

How the Turkey Became a Star

by Tom Pettepiece

Todd was a turkey. But not all the time. Sometimes he was a squirrel and other times he was just a weird stupid jerk.

At least Ralph thought so, because that's what Ralph called Todd every time he saw him. Ralph was a bully.

One day Todd was walking with Nathan on his way to class, when Ralph, who was about a foot taller than Todd, deliberately bumped Todd, as he passed. Everybody saw that Ralph did it on purpose.

"Hey Punk," he said meanly. "Watch where you're going."

Todd tried to ignore him and kept on walking.

"Hey Stupid! Stop when I'm talking to you."

Todd stopped and looked at Nathan. He was scared. Ralph came over and hit Todd on the shoulder as hard as he could. By now, everyone was looking at Todd. He tried, but couldn't hold back the tears. It hurt and worse then that, he felt helpless, alone and humiliated.

"You little wimp," Ralph said. "Look at the crybaby. Crybaby!"

The bell rang. Todd would be late, and everyone would notice he'd been crying.

This sort of thing was common. Every day Ralph did something to Todd. He would sit behind Todd during reading and poke him in the back with a pencil. He'd grab his lunch bag and empty it into the trash while everyone watched.

Occasionally, Todd would say, "Knock it off, Ralph" or "Leave me alone!" but this only seemed to make Ralph more keen to pick on Todd.

The only thing that worked was to stay out of Ralph's way. Todd would plan the time he got to school to miss Ralph before class. At lunch, he'd walk clear around the playground so Ralph couldn't find him.

In short, Todd spent most of his time at school avoiding Ralph. As a result, he made few other friends, was accused of daydreaming by the teacher, missed assignments, and sometimes got poor grades. Ralph was running Todd's life. The only thing that made life bearable was thinking about summer.

☆ ☆

That summer Todd spent several weeks at camp. He created computer games. He learned to spell backwards as fast as he could frontwards. He swam and hiked, and he painted colorful pictures of horses and houses. He sang, acted in skits, and spoke in front of the group. He even learned how to make himself seem heavy or light to pick up, just by picturing in his mind he was an anchor or a feather.

Todd learned that his brain could do amazing things. For the summer, Todd was happy. He felt good about himself and made lots of new friends. The camp was called "Starshine" and Todd was indeed a star!

The day before school started, Todd's mother asked how Todd thought school would be this year. Todd felt anxious. He was already worried about Ralph. But Todd's mother said, "You're a star, Todd. You don't need Ralph calling you names or bothering you again. You're too bright and too confident for that!"

Todd thought about what his mother said, and thought back to all the things he had learned over the summer. He realized that he was strong and capable. He knew that now he had control over how he thought and reacted to things, and that Ralph wasn't going to be able to bully him anymore.

Ralph was there the first day of school, and looked meanly at Todd when they passed in the hallway. But before he could say anything, Todd stopped, smiled confidently and said, "Ralph, don't start anything, because it won't work. You don't have to like me, but it is time you started showing me some respect."

Ralph took a step backwards. He sensed immediately that Todd had changed, and it threw him completely. Ralph mumbled and growled and shuffled his feet, but he couldn't think of anything to say.

Todd stood his ground for a full minute. Finally he said cheerfully, "See ya around, Ralph," and walked away.

Ralph didn't know a lot about respect. Most of what he did know, he had learned the hard way. It took him a long time to understand what he had learned from Todd that day. Though, just to be safe, he steered clear of Todd while he was figuring it out.

Eventually Ralph learned that being courteous and respectful toward people got him all the attention he needed, without the need to constantly prove that he was bigger or tougher than everyone else. He even learned to be friendly.

Four or five years later, when Ralph's bully streak had completely faded away, Todd and Ralph became good friends.

Discussion Questions:

1. How did Ralph's bullying behavior affect Todd?
2. Why didn't Ralph show respect for Todd in the beginning?
3. Do you think Ralph respected himself? Why or why not?
4. What is respectful behavior?
5. Does everyone deserve respect, or is respect something that must be earned?
6. When you loose respect for someone, does that mean that you can treat the person badly? Why or why not?

How the Turkey Became a Star
Experience Sheet

Think about the story of Todd and Ralph. What did you learn from the story? Read and answer the following questions. Be prepared to talk about your answers with a partner or a group of other students.

1. What did Todd learn about himself at camp? _____
_____
_____

2. What did Todd do that helped to change Ralph's attitude toward him?
_____
_____

3. Think of a time when someone bullied you. How did you feel and what did you do?
_____
_____
_____
_____
_____
_____
_____
_____

4. What does it mean to respect someone? _____
_____
_____
_____

5. How do you show respect for others? _____
_____
_____
_____

10. Have you ever lost respect for someone? Without mentioning names, describe what happened.
_____
_____
_____
_____
_____
_____
_____
_____

11. What would it take for you to respect this person again?
_____
_____
_____
_____

Something About Me That's Likable and Worthy of Respect

A Sharing Circle

Objectives:

The students will:
— describe positive qualities in themselves.
— define respect and explain how it is gained.
— compare liking and respecting and identify differences between the two attitudes.

Introduce the Topic:

Each of you is a unique person with many wonderful qualities — qualities that people like and respect. Today we're going to give ourselves credit for some of those qualities. Our topic is, "Something About Me That's Likable and Worthy of Respect."

What is one quality, characteristic, or trait in yourself that you are particularly proud of? Maybe you are a very friendly person, or helpful, or a hard worker. Perhaps people respect the fact that you are reliable, and always keep your promises and commitments. Or maybe your sense of humor is particularly likable. Are you loyal to your friends and family? Are you an understanding, sympathetic, compassionate person? Are you honest and trustworthy? Are you smart, sensible, or logical? Think about your many good qualities for a few moments and tell us about one of them. The topic is, "Something About Me That's Likable and Worthy of Respect."

Discussion Questions:

1. How do you feel when talking about your best qualities?
2. Why is it important to recognize good qualities in ourselves?
3. What does it mean to respect someone?
4. Is it possible to have a trait or quality that is likable, but not respectable? What about respectable, but not likable? Explain.

How I Show Respect Toward Others
A Sharing Circle

Objectives:
The students will:
— identify specific behaviors that show respect.
— explain the difference between feeling respect and demonstrating it.
— state that how they act toward another person is a choice they make.

Introduce the Topic:

Our topic today is about <u>showing</u> respect, which is not the same as <u>having</u> respect. When you have respect for someone, you feel it inside; when you show respect, your actions demonstrate it. Our topic is, "How I Show Respect Toward Others."

Maybe you show your respect for people by being courteous and polite. Another way to show respect is to listen attentively when a person talks and not ridicule or make fun of what he says. Facial expressions can show respect or the lack of it; so can posture, gestures, and other types of body language. At times, showing respect can also mean leaving a person alone, not bothering her, allowing her to believe in, talk about, and do what she thinks is right for her. You might want to picture in your mind someone whom you respect and then think about how you act toward that person that shows your respect. Our topic is, "How I Show Respect Toward Others."

Discussion Questions:

1. What respectful actions were mentioned most during our circle?
2. How do you feel when someone shows respect for you?
3. Why is it important to demonstrate our respect for others?
4. What is the difference between having respect and showing it?
5. Who decides how you will act toward another person?

On the Other Hand

Interviews, Drawing and Discussion

Objectives:

The students will:
— identify respectful actions.
— describe an incident in which they demonstrated respect.
— creatively symbolize expressions of respect.

Materials:

art paper; scratch paper and pencils; colored marker or crayons; glue; decorative materials such as stickers, sequins, buttons, etc. (optional)

Procedure:

Begin by asking the students to think of things that people do to show respect for one another. Focus on small courtesies like greeting a person, saying please and thank you, holding a door, letting someone go first, and shaking hands. Tell the students:

I've heard that some coaches insist that their players shake hands with the members of the opposing team after every game, regardless of whether they win or lose. Why would a coach do that? What message does the coach want to send the other team? What do the players learn by doing this?

After the students have had a few minutes to talk about this display of respect, announce that they are going to participate in an activity about respect, but in this activity instead of shaking hands, they'll draw hands.

Have the students form dyads. Distribute the paper and pencils.

Instruct the students to take turns tracing each other's hand on a sheet of art paper. Point out that the drawing they end up with will be not of their own hand, but of their partner's hand. When they have finished tracing, explain the next step (in your own words):

Interview your partner to find out how your partner shows respect for other people. See if your partner can remember a specific time when he or she said or did something that demonstrated respect for a particular person. Take notes on your scratch paper. Then let your partner interview you. When both of you have finished, use what you've learned to illustrate the tracing of your partner's hand to show the respectful things your partner does. Use letters, symbols, pictures, and other decorations. Your illustration can symbolize lots of respectful actions, or it can tell the story of one particular incident. Decide who will be the first interviewer and get started.

Make available the art materials. List the following questions on the board to assist the students during their interviews:

Interview Questions:

- How do you show respect for other people?
- Can you remember a specific time when you did something for another person that showed respect? What happened?

When the students have finished their drawings, direct each dyad to form a circle with two other dyads. Instruct the students to go around the circle and introduce their partner by showing their hand drawing and describing their partner's respectful actions.

Lead a culminating class discussion.

Discussion Questions:

1. A picture of two hands shaking is often used as a symbol of mutual respect and peace. Why do you think that is?
2. What are some other ways of showing respect that we included in our drawings?
3. If you offered to shake someone's hand and that person refused, what would you think?
4. Why is it important to show respect for others?
5. What would life be like if no one showed respect for anyone else.

The Respectful Classroom
Developing a Classroom Compact

Objectives:
The students will:
— identify specific behaviors that show respect and disrespect.
— explain why respectful behavior is important in the classroom and elsewhere.
— name a series of respectful behaviors that they agree to abide by in the classroom.

Materials:
a picture of a peaceful community, such as a print of the painting *The Peaceable Kingdom* by Edward Hicks, or a community scene done by the master Brueghel, or (for younger children) one of the scenes from a Richard Scarry book, such as *What Do People Do All Day*; chart paper and markers; whiteboard

Procedure:
Show the students a picture of a peaceful community where respect for others is the norm. Ask them: "How does this picture illustrate the theme of respect?"

Spend some time looking at the picture and talking about the cooperative ways in which the characters depicted are interacting. In the process, make sure all of the children understand the meaning of the term *respect*. Cover both the <u>affective/feeling</u> component of respect and its <u>restraining</u> nature.

- regard or esteem for another
- not interfering with or violating another's rights (including the person and his/her property)

Then turn your attention to the classroom. Point out that the classroom is also a community, and that its members should strive to make it a peaceful, respectful one. Discuss what this would be like by asking the students:

—*How would you like to be treated in our classroom?*
—*How would students treat one another in a respectful classroom?*

Next, complete two T-charts like the ones shown on the next page. Develop them one at a time on the board or chart paper. (With older students, discussions may be far ranging, requiring that you develop both simultaneously.) Brainstorm as many items as you can for each list.

Finally, develop a Classroom Compact. Explain to the students that a compact is an agreement or covenant, like the Mayflower Compact written by the pilgrims when they landed in America. Write one or more sentence starters (such as the one shown below) on the board and complete them as a total class. The items that the students list are like rules of conduct, however, be sure to word them in positive, not negative terms. Limit the number of items to no more than six, and make sure everyone agrees on the final list. Appoint a team to create a final version of the Classroom Compact to display in a prominent location. Encourage the team to make the compact colorful and arresting in appearance.

Refer to the Classroom Compact at least once a day. Have regular class meetings to evaluate whether or not the compact is being met. If the students are having trouble abiding by a particular rule, set a goal for the coming week related to improving behavior in that area.

Discussion Questions:

1. How do you feel when someone is disrespectful toward you?
2. How does respectful behavior help the classroom run more smoothly?
3. How can you show respect for others at home? ...in the community?

Respect Looks Like	Respect Sounds Like
Respect Doesn't Look Like	Respect Doesn't Sound Like

Sentence Starter

In this classroom, we treat each other with respect. That means:

1.
2.
3.
4.
5.
6.

This activity was adapted from a similar one developed and described by William J. Kreidler in Instructor, September 1994.

Dear Advice Person
Writing and Discussion

Objectives:
The students will:
— identify disrespectful actions and attitudes in typical situations.
— describe how respectful attitudes require different behaviors in the same situations.

Materials:
sample advice columns from newspapers, magazines, or the internet; one copy of the "Dear Advice Person" letters for each student; writing materials; yellow marking pens (highlighters); bulletin board space

Procedure:

Ask the students if they ever read advice columns. Explain that an advice column is usually written by someone who is considered wise and experienced in a particular area, and is therefore qualified to give advice. Read a few of the inquiries and responses from your sample advice columns. Pass the columns around and distribute the Dear Advice Person letters. Then, in your own words, explain the assignment:

Imagine that you write an advice column for our school newspaper. You have received these three letters from students and must answer them. As you write your responses, try to use the values of respect and self-respect in your answers. Write each response on a separate sheet of paper and sign it "Advice Person."

Collect the responses. Have the students form three groups, and give each group all of the responses to one question, along with a yellow highlighter. Instruct the students to take turns reading the responses and discussing them. Tell them to focus their discussion on the theme of respect, and to use the yellow marking pen to highlight sentences in the response letters that convey good advice about respecting others.

Designate space on a bulletin board for each group to arrange its letter and responses. Conclude with a class discussion.

An excellent way to conclude this activity is with the song, *No One Is a Nobody*. It can also be read as a poem.

Discussion Questions:
1. What was preventing the writers of these letters from showing respect for the people they wrote about?
2. Why is it hard to see things from the other person's point of view?
3. How do you feel when someone doesn't respect your rights?
4. How can we remind ourselves to be aware of the effects our actions have on other people?

Dear Advice Person:

Our neighbor, Mrs. Farrell, gets angry because I turn up my music while I'm doing my yard chores. She says the sound comes right into her house, even when she shuts the windows, and she can't work, or relax, or watch TV or even think. Frankly, I don't think its nearly as bad as she says it is. I've tried to tell her that when I'm working outside, I need to turn the music up so I can hear it over the sound of the tools. Besides, the music makes the time go by faster. But Mrs. Farrell just doesn't understand. What can I do?

Sincerely, *Trying to Keep the Beat*

Dear Advice Person

My grandparents visit us almost every Sunday, and my mom always makes me stop whatever I'm doing and sit around with them for at least an hour while they talk. I love my grandparents, but I don't see why I can't just say hi and maybe stay for 5 minutes. Lots of times I'm out playing with my friends. The other guys make fun of me when I tell them I have to go in because my grandparents are there. What can I do to get my mom to leave me out of it?

Hoping for your reply by the weekend,

Fed Up with Boring Sundays

Dear Advice Person:

My best friend keeps telling me that I ask too many questions. She says that if she wants to tell me something she will, and that I should stop bugging her. She thinks everything is private. But I'm her best friend (she says) and I think best friends should share everything. Sometimes she acts sad or mad about something that happened at home or school. When I ask her about it, she usually just says it was nothing. How can I make her talk to me.

Sincerely, *Wants to Know*

A Big Book of Respect
A Writing and Art Project

Objectives:
The students will:
— describe specific behaviors that demonstrate respect.
— commit to show respect for others in every part of their lives.

Materials:
large sheets of sturdy paper (at least 18 inches by 24 inches); black marking pen; art materials

Procedure:

Prepare a big classroom book with no illustrations (the students will produce these). In large manuscript lettering, write a title on the front cover, such as:

Showing Respect, Day by Day

Write the following text (or your own variation) on the top of each page, leaving plenty of blank space beneath:

Page 1. How I show respect in my family.

Page 2. How I show respect in my school.

Page 3. How I show respect in my neighborhood.

Page 4. How I show respect in my world.

Gather the students together and show them the book. Talk about the meaning of respect and the need to respect others in order to live together peacefully and productively. Tell the students that you have just started the book, and that you need their help to finish it.

Starting with page one, have the students describe specific ways in which they can show respect when they are at home or elsewhere with their family (see sample, next page). Their suggestions will probably be worded in the form of rules. Consider listing the rules on the board during the brainstorming phase, so you can combine and edit somewhat before writing them with a marker on the big-book page. Repeat the process for the remaining pages — school, neighborhood, and world. (You may want to extend this part of the activity over two or more days.)

When the text portion of the book is finished, go back and read through each page with the students and talk about how that page might be illustrated. Brainstorm ideas, make sketches on the board, experiment with composites of several suggestions and, finally, appoint a team of two or three students to render the final illustration.

Display the finished book where the students can thumb through it often. Regularly ask them to commit to demonstrating the behaviors they listed in all four environments. Feature the book at parent visitations.

Discussion Questions:

1. Which of the respectful behaviors we listed do you sometimes have trouble with?
2. How can you work on developing more respect in that area?
3. How can we help each other show respect in the classroom?
4. How would our classroom be different if everyone always followed the rules we listed?

Variation:

Have the students do the writing. Instead of listing the rules yourself, have the students take turns writing rules on the page. Students could also be appointed to do the cover and page headings.

How I show respect in my family.

I listen when people talk to me.

I do my chores.

I help keep the house clean.

I don't argue with my parents.

I behave well when we go out.

I say please and thank you.

I don't interrupt.

A Web of Respect
Game, Discussion, and Poetry Reading

Objectives:
The students will:
— create a symbolic expression of their connectedness.
— describe positive qualities that they respect in one another.
— explain how the actions of one person in a group affect the actions of everyone else.

Materials:
a large ball of string; a copy of Chief Seattle's poem for each student (see below) or the poem written on the board

Procedure:
Have the students sit on the floor in a large circle. Determine which student's birthday is closest to the present date. Confer on that student both the ball of string and the honor of starting the activity. Instruct the student to grasp the end of the string and hold it while throwing the ball across the circle to another student.

Next, direct the student who threw the ball to say something positive about the student who catches it. In your own words, elaborate:

Look directly at the student who catches the ball of string, and describe <u>one</u> thing you respect and appreciate about that person. If you think he or she is friendly, humorous, athletic, helpful, loyal, musically talented, has nice hair, is a math whiz, or has a great smile — say that to the person. The "catcher" must accept the positive statement and can say "thank you" or "thanks," but nothing else. Holding onto the string, the catcher then throws the ball to another person in the circle and repeats the process. When it's your turn to throw the ball, you can aim at a specific person, but you must accept and speak to whomever catches the ball. With our throwing skills, we should be able to include everyone, with no repeats, the first time around.

Make sure the students continue to hold onto their portion of the string, keeping it fairly taut. When everyone has had at least one turn to throw and catch, and a web has been formed that connects everyone in the circle, tell the students that you would like to read them a poem written one and a half centuries ago by a Native American chief. Slowly read the poem at the bottom of the next page:

Give the students an opportunity to respond to the poem and its meaning. You may want to read it a second time. Then, direct the group to stand up carefully. Admire the web for a few final moments before asking the last person (the one holding the ball) to move around the group and rewind the string. If you have made handouts of the poem, distribute them. Otherwise, direct the attention of the students to the poem copied on the board. Refer to the poem while leading a final discussion.

Discussion Questions:
1. What does this poem say about respecting the earth and everything on the earth? Does that include people? Explain.
2. What is meant by the words, *All things are bound together. All things connect*?
3. In what ways are all of us in this class connected?
4. How are we connected to the rest of the school? ...the community? ...the nation? ...the earth?
5. What is meant by, *Whatever he does to the web, he does to himself*?
6. Can you describe an example showing how what one person in our class does affects everyone else?

All things are bound together.

All things connect.

What happens to the Earth

Happens to the children of the Earth.

Man has not woven the web of life.

He's but one thread.

Whatever he does to the web

He does to himself.

—Chief Seattle, 1856

NO ONE IS A NOBODY

(1)
I'm lovable and capable and I know that you are, too.
I'm unique; there's only one me.
You're unique; there's only one you. In fact...

CHORUS
No one is a nobody. Each person's important, you see.
Each one has rights and feelings and dreams;
What happens to you will change other lives, too.

No one is a nobody. Each person's important, you see.
Each one I meet as I walk down the street
Is just as special as I am.

(2)
Sometimes I don't feel too lovable
Or very capable, either.
Then someone comes along and shows me that they care.
It reminds me that I do matter after all. It's true that...

CHORUS

(3)
Other times I forget about your rights,
And that you have feelings, too.
And the world doesn't spin for just me; it's true.
If I care for myself, I'll care for you. Because...

CHORUS

Music is available, as a download, from www.songsforteaching.com

Copyright © 1996 by Linda K. Williams

Service to Others

Story:

Marvin's Last Invention
Experience Sheet

Sharing Circles:

Something Nice I Did for a Friend
What I Wish I Could Do to Make This a Better World

Activities:

New-Kid Survival Kits
A School Service Project

Senior Visits and Gift Baskets
A Community Service Activity

No More Litter
An Environmental Awareness Activity

Organ Donation Compaign
A National Health Service Project

Song/Poem:

Ripples and Starfish

Marvin's Last Invention
by Tom Pettepiece

Marvin was always inventing something strange.

Once he invented a bubble gum that lasted four days without losing its flavor. Another time he invented a machine that let you eat dinner, listen to your parents and do your homework all at once so you'd have more time to play.

Half of what he invented never worked, and most of the kids thought he was crazy. But this, he thought, was his best invention yet — the "Deluxe Wish-A-World."

The Wish-A-World was secretly hooked up to the classroom computer. Marvin entered the name of any book in the school library and a page number, and one day later, whatever object or topic was being discussed on that page, anywhere in the world, would appear.

He tested it with the book *How Things Work*, page 46, about how pencils are made. In the morning his desk was stuffed with bright new yellow unsharpened pencils — enough for the whole school!

"Wonderful!" he blurted out in the middle of silent reading. Marvin could hardly believe it! Fortunately, no one paid any attention because everyone had come to accept Marvin's outbursts of strange behavior as normal for someone who seemed to spend as much time daydreaming as Marvin.

Marvin quickly got the encyclopedia and turned to "G." He was going to become rich overnight by materializing "gold." He hastily typed in the encyclopedia's name, volume number 7 and page 314, and set the machine to work. That night he hardly slept, bursting with excitement.

When Marvin got to school the next day, there was a giant commotion. Police cars, and ambulances filled the parking lot. Paramedics, the Red Cross, doctors, nurses, and scores of other people were rushing in and out of the school buildings. He thought there had been some sort of accident until he got closer and saw that inside the school were hundreds and hundreds of children from all over the world, dressed in every kind of clothing imaginable and speaking different languages. It was mass confusion!

In his haste to enter his request for "gold" Marvin had left out a digit in the page number. Instead of reading 314, it read 34, the page for "Children." There were so many children in the school that there was no room to walk! And the worst part of it was that over half of them were either starving or sick.

Teams of parents and community volunteers had been called to bring in food and water. Most of the hungry children were not even five-years old. Nurses were there to give them shots because many of the children were sick with diseases that kids in the United States rarely got anymore, and if they didn't get treatment fast, some were going to die!

Marvin was white as a sheet with

fright! What had he done? After he figured out that his machine was somehow responsible for the mess, he thought of telling his teacher, but got scared when he heard the principal shout, "Who's responsible for this? They're in big trouble!"

The sick and hungry children were from the poor countries that made up over half of the world. Some of their homes had been bombed in wars. Others were poor because pollution or lack of rain had made it impossible for their families to grow food. And still others were from overcrowded cities where they had been sleeping in the street and begging.

It was pitiful and Marvin felt sick. Not only had he created problems for his school, the needs of these children seemed impossible to meet. And how would he ever send them back! The machine was only for getting things, not giving them back. Marvin thought he would be expelled from school for the next 100 years!

But as he watched, a strange thing happened. After the initial shock, people seemed to be happily working together. For all the trouble they went through to get food, medicine, and clothing for the children, they were enjoying themselves! And no one seemed mad! In fact, someone said, "We've got more than enough here. I'm glad these children can use it."

Marvin woke with a start. "What a dream!" he said to himself. He got dressed and ran to school without even having breakfast. As soon as the bell rang, he dashed into the room and turned off his machine. Luckily, he stopped it before anything appeared.

When the teacher began the social studies lesson for the day, Marvin raised his hand impatiently. "I've got a great idea," he said. "Why don't we make a project of studying how children live in other countries and maybe even raise some money to send them so they won't be so hungry!"

The class was stunned. Not only did Marvin rarely speak in class, he almost never made sense when he did.

"Good idea!" said the teacher with a puzzled look on his face. The class agreed.

Marvin's "Deluxe Wish-A-World" machine never did work after that, but he didn't care. Marvin got so involved in the project that he forgot about inventing crazy things. Instead, he invented more ways to help children all over the world get what they wished for.

Discussion Questions:

1. Why did Marvin turn off the machine before the gold appeared?
2. Why were most of the children hungry or sick? Name some of the countries the children may have come from.
3. Why didn't Marvin invent any more crazy things?
4. What made the class decide to accept Marvin's idea to study about and help children?
5. Why is it important to help others?
6. What are some ways that people can be of service to our community? ...to the nation? ...the world?
7. What would things be like if no one helped anyone else?

Marvin's Last Invention
Experience Sheet

Think about the story of Marvin, his inventions, and his dream. Then answer these questions:

1. What did Marvin realize about the children of the world when he saw them in his dream? What made him want to help them?

_____
_____
_____
_____

2. Think of a time when you performed some kind of service for another person, a group, or the community. It could have been something as small as picking up some litter, or it could have been a major project. What did you do and how did you feel about it?

_____
_____
_____
_____

2. How do you benefit personally from being of service to others? What do you get out of it?

_____
_____
_____
_____
_____

Something Nice I Did for a Friend

A Sharing Circle

Objectives:

The students will:
— describe ways of being of service to others.
— discuss how thoughtful deeds benefit both giver and receiver.

Introduce the Topic:

Our topic for this session is, "Something Nice I Did for a Friend." Friends do thoughtful things for each other all the time. That's part of what builds friendship. Tell us something that you did for one of your friends. It doesn't have to be something spectacular — small deeds are important, too. For example, maybe you accompanied your friend to the library and helped her find some books for a report. Perhaps you offered to feed your friend's pet while he was on vacation. Or maybe you were a good listener when your friend was feeling sad or upset about something. Have you ever drawn a picture or made a little gift for a friend? Have you ever given a friend a funny card? There are many thoughtful things we can do for our friends. Tell us about one. The topic is, "Something Nice I Did for a Friend."

Discussion Questions:

1. How did you feel when you did the thoughtful thing you described?
2. How do you feel when your friends do nice things for you?
3. Why is it important to take the time to give thoughtful service to others?

What I Wish I Could Do to Make This a Better World

A Sharing Circle

Objectives:

The students will:
— identify global problems that need to be addressed.
— explain that they have a relationship to the planet and all its people.

Introduce the Topic:

Our topic today allows us to think big and not worry about whether or not something is truly possible. We're going to talk about the way we <u>wish</u> things could be. The topic is, "What I Wish I Could Do to Make This a Better World."

If you could do anything you wished to make the world a better place, what would it be? What service would you give to the whole world? Maybe you'd give every kid in the world a happy home with a loving family. Or maybe you'd send food to all parts of the world where people are hungry. Or perhaps your wish would be to give all people a good education so that they could be productive and successful. Maybe you'd make the world a better place by getting rid of pollution, or showing people how to settle conflicts peacefully, or giving everyone the ability to speak and understand many languages so they could communicate better. Or you might choose to make the world a better place by doing something fun. Maybe you'd build a Disneyland in every country, or hook up the whole world and play a computer game involving every country. Use your imagination and tell us what you would do. The topic is, "What I Wish I Could Do to Make This a Better World."

Discussion Questions:

1. Which of our ideas might really be possible? How might they be accomplished?
2. Why is it important to think about the well being of the whole world? Why can't we just worry about ourselves?
3. What are some things that we can do to make the world a better place?

New-Kid Survival Kits
A School Service Project

Objectives:
The students will:
— identify the needs/desires of new students.
— creatively compile information and services to meet the needs of new students.

Materials:
multiple copies of an appropriate organizer, e.g., inexpensive 3-ring binders, expandable file folders, large envelopes, presentation folders with pockets, etc.; art materials

Procedure:

Begin this activity by asking the students: *What is it like to be a new kid at school? How many of you have had that experience?*

Invite volunteers to share what it's like to enter a new school where you don't know anyone. Ask them if anyone showed them around during the first week or so, and whether or not the staff and students were welcoming and friendly. Point out that one of the nicest things they can do is to make a new student feel a part of the school from the very first day.

Announce that, as a service project, the students are going to prepare "survival kits" to give to new students.

As a total group, brainstorm the contents of the kit. Try to think of as many things as possible that a new student might find useful or encouraging. Follow the rules of brainstorming, i.e., anything goes, be creative, no evaluation during the brainstorming process, no put downs of any kind. Your list might include:

- a map of the school
- information about the school (description, history, unique characteristics, special relationships, e.g., with local colleges or businesses)
- a school district telephone directory (perhaps an abbreviated version)
- a school calendar, with special events marked
- a student handbook or list of rules/requirements
- information about teachers (names, classes, room numbers)
- information about office staff
- lists of sports, service groups, and clubs, with information on how they are organized and how to become involved
- descriptions of future school events, including dates and times
- location of lost and found
- jokes, cartoons, or stories authored by students

- student-made coupons redeemable for special services, e.g., a campus tour, help with homework, introductions to six kids, a recess game partner, etc.
- a copy of the student newspaper
- PTA information
- a map of the town or city
- names and telephone numbers of local medical facilities
- coupons for treats at local stores and businesses
- information about public transportation
- a candy bar or treat

After the brainstorming process is concluded, go back and evaluate the list, narrow it down and make final selections.

Choose teams of volunteers to obtain or prepare the various items needed. When everything has been collected, appoint an "assembly team" to:
1. Decide on the best presentation of the items.
2. Put together a model kit
3. Design and produce a cover
3. Develop a system for efficiently assembling the kits.

Appoint another team to answer distribution questions. Have them consider the pros and cons of several distribution alternatives. For example:
- Assign a person to hand deliver each kit and perhaps act as a companion/guide throughout the first day.
- Mail the kit.
- Deliver the kit to the home of the new student.
- Give out kits at a monthly "newcomers" reception or party.

When the kits are finished and all of the decisions regarding distribution have been made, facilitate a culminating discussion.

Discussion Questions:

1. How do you feel when you do something to help a person you don't yet know?
2. How would you feel if a friendly student presented you with a kit like this when you entered a new school?
3. How do we benefit from reaching out to others?

Senior Visits and Gift Baskets

A Community Service Activity

Objectives:
The students will:
— identify the needs of seniors living in a managed-care environment.
— create and assemble gifts for the seniors.
— spend time interacting with the recipients of the gift baskets.

Materials:
a variety of gift items; suitable containers; wrapping and decorating materials

Procedure:

This is a perfect activity for the holidays, but is needed and appreciated all year long.

Have the students research the nursing homes, senior centers, and retirement homes in your area. Ask them to find out:
— the number of residents
— the general health of residents
— recreational and personal-care needs
— whether the administration would welcome visits and gifts from children
— the best times of the day for visits

Based on this information, choose the most compatible senior residence. Then telephone that organization and obtain more specific suggestions concerning what to include in gift baskets. If the resident population is greater than the number of baskets you plan to make, ask the administrator to select individuals who especially need and would appreciate the service. If possible, obtain a list of names so that the students can label the baskets. Calendar a date and time for the class to visit.

Prepare the baskets. Finalize a list of items. Possibilities include:
- personal grooming supplies (combs, brushes, toothpaste, shampoo, deodorant, mirrors, lipstick)
- food (fruit, nuts, candy, muffins, cookies, breads)
- clothing
- sheets, pillowcases, or blankets
- flowers (potted plants, silk arrangements, fresh)
- letters and cards
- videos, and compact disks (used CDs are very inexpensive and never wear out)
- books

Decide what kind of container will best hold the contents of the gift baskets. You may use actual baskets (natural or synthetic) or you may find that boxes, gift bags, or bags that the students decorate themselves work better.

Hold a fund-raiser to raise money for the gifts, or circulate a flyer describing the project and listing of needed items. Ask students and staff members to contribute one new item.

Have teams of students assemble the gift baskets and wrap or decorate them.

Talk to the senior organization to find out what other activities the students can do with the residents during their visit. For example, they might:
— perform a skit
— lead some sing-a-longs
— play games
— lead simple stretching and movement exercises
— teach the seniors a dance (wheelchairs can dance, too)

Brief the students about appropriate behavior during their visit. In particular, make them aware of the physical limitations of the people they'll be visiting, and share any specific guidelines provided by the administrator of the senior residence.

After the visit, lead the class in a follow-up discussion. If you like, wrap up the discussion by singing the song, "Ripples and Starfish." Before teaching the song, take a few minutes to compose a simple tune to fit the lyrics. The music is also available as a download from www.songsforteaching.com. The words may also be read as a poem.

Discussion Questions:
1. What was the best part of this activity for you?
2. How did giving to the seniors cause you to feel? How do you think the seniors felt?
3. Would you like to visit the center again? What ideas do you have for another visit?

Extension:

Be ready to sponsor an "Adopt a Senior" or "Adopt a Grandfriend" program for students who respond particularly well to this activity. Turn a single visit into a long-term commitment by each student to visit, share, and support one particular senior.

No More Litter
An Environmental Awareness Activity

Objectives:
The students will:
— develop and present anti-littering posters
— explain that littering can be reduced through awareness of the problem and taking steps to prevent it
— state that litter is unsightly, dangerous and is costly to clean up

Materials:
poster-size art paper, magic markers, assorted art supplies such as colored paper; cloth; glue; optional litter items such as styrofoam cups, cigarette butts, candy wrappers, plastic bags, 6-pack rings, etc.

Procedure:

Develop interest in the topic of litter by asking the students, *What's wrong with litter?* Listen to their responses, use the student's comments to lead a discussion incorporating the following points: Litter is illegal. Litter is dirty. Not only does it look ugly but it can carry germs. Some animals are attracted to litter and pick up germs from it, and they can get sick or carry the germs to people.

Litter is bad for the environment. It can get washed down into storm drains and be carried into rivers and lakes and oceans. Sometimes litter is dumped directly into water where it can be dangerous to birds and fish. The water can also become polluted and no longer safely be used for drinking and recreation.

Litter also costs lots of money to clean up and when cans and bottles are not recycled, more resources and money must be used to create cans and bottles from new resources.

If computers are available have the students extend their knowledge of the problem of littering by doing internet research.

Direct the students to form partnerships and to select either a problem that littering causes or a remedy of what they should do with trash. Say to the students: *You and your partner will do the best job you can to teach the rest of us about littering. As a team create a poster that shows either a problem that littering causes or a solution to the problem of littering. See how clearly and cleverly you can get your point across. Do this by combining words and illustrations. Use any of the art materials provided.* Tell the students how long you will give them to create their posters and when they will make a presentation to the rest of the class.

Make the art materials available to the students and encourage them to add their own embellishments, including the "litter items". Circulate as they work and answer questions and help as needed.

When the posters have been completed, have the teams prepare a brief presentation to show their poster and to tell the rest of the class about it. Provide time for all the teams to present either immediately following the creation of the posters or at another designated time.

After the students have made their presentations, discuss their reactions to the information gained. Ask these and your own discussion questions.

Discussion Questions:

1. What has been the most interesting or surprising thing you've learned about the problem of littering?
2. How can each of us prevent littering?
3. How does littering affect many more people than just the person who litters?

Extensions:

- Display completed posters on bulletin boards and in other locations around the class and/or school.

- Have the students give their presentation on littering prevention to other classrooms.

Organ Donation Campaign
A National Health Service Project

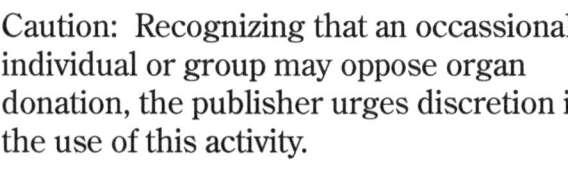

Objectives:
The students will:
— explain the purpose, procedures, and benefits of organ donation.
— develop and implement ways to increase the number of donors in the community.
— practice planning and organizing skills.

Caution: Recognizing that an occassional individual or group may oppose organ donation, the publisher urges discretion in the use of this activity.

Materials:
organ donor cards available from the National Kidney Foundation, www.kidney.org, from many motor vehicle departments, the American Heart Association, or the transplant coordinators of nearby hospitals; other materials dictated by specific campaign strategies.

Procedure:
Talk to the students about the need for donor organs to save and/or prolong the lives of people suffering from kidney, lung, heart, liver and other diseases. Make these points:

- Organ transplantation is widely used as a means to prolong life and improve the quality of life for individuals who have diseased and failing hearts, lungs, kidneys or livers. Hospitals in most major cities now have skilled surgical and support teams who specialize in transplanting one or more organs.

- The number of people who need organs and are eligible for them is much greater than the number of organs available.

- To become an organ donor, an adult simply signs and carries an organ donor card, usually next to his/her driver's license. In addition, a person should ask his/her family to honor the decision. (Even if a person is carrying a donor card, the family is *always* asked for permission before the organs of a deceased person are used for transplantation.)

- Donor organs are removed from deceased donors after they die. Removal is accomplished through careful surgical procedures and the body is never disfigured or treated dishonorably. Some organs are donated by living persons. For example, people can give one of their kidneys to a relative.

- Patients who receive donated organs are chosen in a fair way through a

national computer network. Selection is made based on blood/tissue (genetic) matching, length of time on the waiting list, and geographical location. (Organs can often be packed in ice and flown across country, but this is avoided if a suitable recipient is found in the same or a nearby community.)
- It costs nothing to donate an organ. The family of the deceased is never asked to pay a penny for the surgical or medical procedures.
- Organ donation is enthusiastically supported by many religious organizations and no major religions oppose it. (A few choose to remain neutral.)
- A way to <u>save lives</u> is to increase the number of organ donors — people who carry donor cards (and have talked with their families).

Engage the students in planning and conducting an organ donor campaign in your community. Have them begin by writing or faxing a letter requesting a supply of organ donor cards.

If a transplant program exists at a hospital in your area, invite a transplant coordinator to visit your class and make a presentation. Coordinators are highly skilled at explaining organ donation and will be able to give the class many helpful hints about how to conduct a campaign.

Here are some suggestions for campaign strategies:
- Have selected students develop presentations for other classes and the PTA.
- Make posters about organ donation and display them at school and in stores and businesses around the community. Include a supply of donor cards.
- Work cooperatively with organizations planning special events, such as concerts, craft fairs, and community celebrations. Set up a booth at the event, or distribute organ donor cards at ticket booths.
- Develop a skit or short dramatic presentation on the theme of organ donation and present it at assemblies, PTA, and community events.
- Identify individuals in your community who have received transplanted organs. Many recipients are eager to tell their stories to help the cause of organ donation. Have them speak to the children and invite them to be featured speakers at campaign events.

Throughout this activity, take advantage of learning opportunities related to science, health, social studies, careers and math. Have the students work in teams throughout the campaign, practicing step-by-step problem-solving and planning procedures. Debrief these processes regularly, helping the students internalize organizational and leadership skills. Facilitate a class discussion following every major event or stage of the campaign.

Discussion Questions:

1. In what ways is this activity helping our community? ...nation? ...you?
2. What are some of the ways that both donors and recipients benefit from organ donation?
3. What do you think will be possible in the future as the science of organ donation advances?
4. How well did your team work together during this event/process? What problems did you encounter and how did you solve them?
5. What are some of the steps you should take when planning an event or campaign like this?

RIPPLES AND STARFISH
A Song of Empowerment

REFRAIN:
Like ripples and starfish, ripples and starfish, I know that
One by one, our words and deeds can build a better world!

(1)
When one of Gandhi's followers felt his efforts made no difference at all,
Gandhi said to him, "Your words and actions matter, whether large or small.
"You need to choose them with great care. They're like pebbles that you cast into a pond.
"The ripples will take care of themselves, I've found."

REFRAIN

(2)
The man on the beach was working earnestly to throw the stranded starfish back into the sea
When someone laughed at him and said, "You'll never save them all, don't you see?"
This bothered him not; he continued on, and threw another one to safety.
His answer was, "Well, I made a difference to that one, certainly."

REFRAIN

(3)
So instead of cursing the darkness, I'll light a candle to brighten the way.
When others see my flickering flame, surely many will add a shining ray.
So though the task may seem without end, we'll start to make a difference today;
We know not where our ripples will end, but we'll send them on their way.

REFRAIN

FINAL, MODIFIED REFRAIN
Like ripples and starfish, ripples and starfish, I know that
One by one, if we lend a hand . . .
One by one, if we take a stand . . .
Yes, one by one our words and deeds can build a better world . . .
Build a better world!

Music is available, as a download, from www.songsforteaching.com

Copyright 1996 by Linda K. Williams

Responsibility

Story:

Anna and the Silver Bracelet
Experience Sheet

Sharing Circles:

I Stopped Myself from Damaging Someone's Property
A Time I Helped Without Being Asked

Activities:

Responsibility Log
A Student Self-Assessment

Learning to Set Goals
Experience Sheet and Discussion

I Depend on You, You Depend on Me
Experience Sheet and Discussion

Framing the Blame Game
Cartooning and Discussion

Striving for Excellence
Skits, Discussion and Song

Song:

Who I Am Makes a Difference

Anna and the Silver Bracelet
by Dianne Schilling

"Hurry up, Lynette," said Anna impatiently. "The bell's about to ring. We'll be late, and Mr. Garcia will get grouchy."

"Okay, okay," replied Lynette, grabbing a paper towel from the holder in the corner. "I'm washing my hands — like a good girl."

Anna pushed through the door expecting Lynette to follow. But as she stepped into the sunshine, she heard Lynette — still in the bathroom — cry out, "Wow! Come look at this, Anna!"

Anna sighed and retraced her steps into the girl's bathroom. Lynette was still standing next to the towel holder. "Look what I found. It was on the floor behind the trash can," she exclaimed excitedly. She held up something shiny and silver. Anna couldn't tell what it was.

"Great," said Anna. "I'm going to class." With that she was out the door and heading down the outside hall at top speed. Lynette had to run to catch up.

"Isn't it beautiful?" Lynette said, juggling her pack with one hand while admiring the silver thing in the other.

"What is it?" asked Anna. She was more interested in reaching the classroom before the bell rang than looking at Lynette's treasure.

"A bracelet, silly. I think it's real silver."

"I wonder who lost it," said Anna, just as they reached the classroom door. "Whew, we made it."

The shrill bell sounded just as Anna turned the knob. She held the door so Lynette could enter, and watched her friend quickly shove the silver bracelet into a jeans pocket. Anna was surprised. Kids were supposed to turn in found items to their teacher or the office. Oh well, Lynette was probably waiting till later.

Jeff walked part way home with Anna and Lynette. He kept the girls in stitches with funny stories about the new puppies at his house. His mother was a breeder of Siberian Huskies, so daily Jeff had some new mischief to report.

As soon as Jeff turned down Tower Street and the two girls were climbing the hill to their own block, Lynette withdrew the silver bracelet from her pocket. She held it up so the sun reflected off the smooth metal. Then she let it slip down over her wrist and admired it against her skin.

"Why didn't you turn it in?" asked Anna, trying not to sound accusing.

"Oh, I don't know. Just forgot, I guess," said Lynette dreamily. A moment later she added, "But I will," before dropping the bracelet into her book pack.

As always, they reached Anna'a house first. Anna trudged up the walk and turned at the door to wave and watch as Lynette climbed the hill to her own home at the end of the street.

The next afternoon, as he did almost every afternoon, Mr. Garcia spent a few minutes reading aloud the office bulletin. The bulletin contained announcements about special events, changes in the school calendar, reminders of club meetings, and — occasionally — one or two lost-and-found items.

"A silver bracelet with an engraved flower design was lost at school on Tuesday. If you find it or have any information, talk to the secretary, Mrs. Peterson," read Mr. Garcia.

Anna shot a questioning look at Lynette who was working quietly in the back of the room. Lynette didn't look up.

When Mr. Garcia finished the bulletin, he moved right into a social studies lesson, and then a writing assigment, and then cooperative group projects. Anna wanted to talk to Lynette about the bracelet, but she never had a chance. After school she waited by the elm tree at the corner of the playground, but Lynette never showed up, so Anna walked home alone.

Anna had trouble concentrating on her homework. Images of the shiny silver bracelet kept popping into her mind. Mostly she thought about the bracelet on her friend's wrist. Lynette loved jewelry and it was easy to see she was crazy about that bracelet. Was she planning to keep it?

Anna decided to find out. Feeling nervous but determined, she went to the kitchen phone, picked up the handset and punched in Lynette's number. Lynette's brother answered and called to his sister. When she picked up the phone, Lynette sounded breathless and cheerful. "Hi, sorry you had to walk home alone. I forgot to tell you my mom was picking me up for a dentist appointment."

"Yuck," said Anna, with a shiver. "The last time I went to the dentist I had to have two fillings. I hate that awful sound, and the shots hurt. Did you have to have shots?" The purpose of Anna's call was momentarily washed beneath a wave of sympathy.

"No," said Lynette. "But I don't like it either, and anyway let's not talk about dentists. Wasn't Henry funny at lunch today? I wish he could be in our class."

The girls talked about their friends and boys and family outings. Finally Anna remembered why she called and asked, "Lynette, did you turn in the bracelet?"

Silence.

"Lynette? Are you there?"

Finally, her voice shaking, Lynette said slowly, "Anna, I told you I was going to turn it in. Just don't bug me about it, okay?"

"But have you turned it in?" persisted Anna.

"No, not yet. I keep forgetting. What's the matter, don't you trust me? Anyway, it's none of your business!" Now Lynette's voice sounded angry.

"But it doesn't belong to you Lynette, and somebody feels bad because it's gone. How would you feel if..."

Anna heard a 'click' and realized that Lynette had hung up. She felt awful and wondered if she was being a bad friend.

She thought about calling Lynette back and apologizing, but decided against it. Maybe she should just mind her own business.

But minding her own business was tough for Anna. Especially when "lost bracelet" posters began to show up around school. She saw one on a bulletin board outside the main office and another taped to the side of a classroom building. She practically ran into one stapled to a utility pole on the edge of the playground.

The more she thought about it, the more Anna realized that the lost bracelet was her business. After all, she was there when Lynette found it. She saw Lynette put the bracelet in her pocket. And Lynette was her best friend — though, come to think of it, she wasn't acting very friendly these days.

A couple of afternoons later during recess, Anna and Lynette were playing on the bars with several other girls, when someone mentioned the lost bracelet.

"My mom won't let me wear my nice stuff to school," said one girl, "It's too easy to lose."

"Yea, and who's going to turn in a bracelet like that? Most kids would keep it," said another.

"Finders keepers, losers weepers," chanted Lynette. The other girls laughed.

Anna couldn't believe her ears. Lynette really did plan to keep the bracelet, and not only that — she thought it was okay! Right then and there, Anna made up her mind to visit the school counselor.

Ms. Elliott was one of Anna's favorite people at school. She was friendly and helpful, and when Anna's grandfather died last year, Ms. Elliott and Anna talked several times, sometimes taking long walks around the neighborhood near the school.

When Anna knocked on the side of her open office door, Ms. Elliott looked up and smiled brightly. "Hi, Anna," she said. "Come in and sit down. I haven't had a visit from you in a long time. I hear you're doing well in class. Why don't you bring me up to date."

They chatted about school and about Anna's family. Anna felt nervous and the pleasant conversation calmed her. After a few minutes, Ms. Elliott paused and asked, "Did you have a special reason for dropping by today, Anna?" Anna nodded and stared at the floor. Ms. Elliott waited.

Finally, Anna blurted out, "I know who has the lost bracelet. I saw her pick it up off the floor of the bathroom and put in her pocket. I don't think she's going to turn it in."

Anna told Ms. Elliott the whole story. She explained that keeping the secret was making her feel bad, and she expressed her confusion over what to do. She wanted to be loyal to her best friend, but didn't think it was right for Lynette to keep something that didn't belong to her. Ms. Elliott listened. She let Anna know that she understood how hard it was tell on a friend. In the end, though, Ms. Elliott stressed that Anna was feeling badly because she was going against her own conscience.

"Pretending you don't know anything about the bracelet is not a responsible thing to do," said Ms. Elliott seriously. "Your conscience won't let you be like an ostrich who sticks her head in the sand. It wants you to be a responsible person, and there are only two ways to do that. Either convince Lynette that she must return the bracelet, or report what you know."

"But Lynette will hate me," worried Anna.

"Maybe not," said Ms. Elliott. "You don't know how Lynette really feels about keeping the bracelet. I'll bet that deep down, she has just as many doubts as you."

Anna felt better when she left Ms. Elliott's office. She decided to try that afternoon, one more time, to talk some sense into Lynette.

But when Jeff turned off at Tower Street and the two girls were climbing the hill, Anna didn't know how to begin her confrontation, so she said instead, "That's a cool jacket, Lynette. Is it new?"

"Isn't it great! My dad bought it for me on a business trip. Everybody kept coming up to me all day, telling me how much they liked it. It's the neatest jacket I've ever had!" exclaimed Lynette, proudly.

A little light bulb flickered in Anna's brain. "You probably shouldn't wear it to school," she said, watching Lynette's reaction.

"Why not? shrugged Lynette, "It's been cold lately."

Anna focused on the sidewalk and tried to speak casually. "Because if you ever lay it on a bench, or hang it over the back of a chair in the cafeteria, or leave it on a hook in the bathroom, you'll probably never see it again."

Lynette's steps slowed, but she didn't say anything, so Anna plunged ahead.

"Whoever finds it will think it's cool and keep it," she said.

"They wouldn't do that," protested Lynette.

"Sure they will. They'll say 'finders keepers' and they won't worry about you at all," insisted Anna.

Suddenly Lynette stopped. "I know why you're saying this to me, Anna, and it's a mean thing to do. You're hoping someone will take my jacket because of the bracelet. If you care so much about that old bracelet, why don't you find out who lost it and be her friend! I don't want you for a friend anymore!"

Anna stood alone at her front gate, watching Lynette storm up the hill. She felt sad and fought the urge to cry.

The sadness grew as afternoon turned to evening and smells of dinner drifted through the house. Anna wasn't hungry. She knew she was going to have to tell on Lynette and it made her feel queazy. She picked her way through the meal, trying to act normal, did her homework and slept fitfully.

Anna didn't expect to see Lynette the next morning, so she was surprised when her "ex-friend" showed up at the front gate 15 minutes earlier than usual. Nervously, Anna walked to the gate. "Hi," she said. "I didn't think you'd want to walk together today, and anyway I'm not quite ready." Anna noticed that Lynette was not wearing her new jacket. She was wearing the silver bracelet.

"I'm sorry about yesterday," said Lynette sheepishly. "I thought about what you said all night. I realized that if someone found my jacket and kept it, I'd think they were the worst person in the world. The more I thought about it, the more I felt like the worst person in the world."

Anna was so relieved her knees started to shake.

Lynette took off the bracelet and held it out to Anna. "Here," she said. "Take it. I never really wanted it. ...Well, maybe I did at first, but not for long. Will you turn it in for me?"

Anna shook her head firmly. "No, Lynette," she said, "you have to do it. You were the one who found it and you were the one who kept it all this time, so you're the one who has to turn it in."

"But I'm scared," pleaded Lynette. "That's why I didn't take it back. I was just admiring it in my drawer, and I kept putting it off. Then after a few days I couldn't take it back because it would look like I was planning to keep it. It's really stupid, but I don't know how to explain it!"

"You can say exactly what you said to me," suggested Anna. "I talked to Ms. Elliott about it, and she said we'll feel better if we take responsiblity for our actions. I think she's right."

"We?" questioned Lynette.

"Yes, we," repeated Anna. "I knew you had the bracelet all this time, and I didn't say anything until I talked to Ms. Elliott. Of course, she didn't report it. She's a counselor. She just put it back on me. So I have to go with you and take responsibility for playing dumb."

"Really? You'll go with me?" said Lynette hopefully.

"Sure," said Anna. "You'll see, — it won't be so bad. Wait while I get my things and we'll go do it right now."

Anna ran in the house and was back in less than two minutes, breathlessly stumbling through the gate. The two friends threw their arms around each other and hugged. Laughing, they headed down the hill.

"Come on," said Lynette. "Let's get this over with!"

Discussion Questions:

1. What's wrong with keeping a lost item that you happen to find?
2. Why did Lynette wait to turn in the bracelet?
3. Why was she afraid to turn it in later?
4. Why did Anna feel that turning in the bracelet was her responsibility, too?
5. What does it mean to be a responsible person?
6. What does it mean to take responsibility for your actions?

Anna and the Silver Bracelet
Experience Sheet

Think about the story of Anna, whose friend found a bracelet and almost kept it. Write your answers to these questions:

1. Have you ever lost something and gotten it back because the person who found it was responsible and honest? Describe what happened:

   _____
   _____
   _____

2. Have you ever found something and turned it in? Why did you turn in the item, and how did you feel about your actions?

   _____
   _____
   _____

3. You've probably heard the saying, "Finders keepers, losers weepers." Maybe you've even said it yourself. What's wrong with the ideas behind that saying?

   _____
   _____
   _____
   _____

I Stopped Myself from Damaging Someone's Property

A Sharing Circle

Objectives:

The students will:
— state the importance of respecting the property of others.
— describe incidents in which they took responsibility for their own actions, even in the face of peer pressure.

Introduce the Topic:

Today, our topic is about vandalism, which is the act of damaging another person's property. We're going to discuss times when we came close to being vandals ourselves. The topic is, "I Stopped Myself from Damaging Someone's Property."

Can you remember a time when you almost did something to a person's property that would have made it less valuable or worthless, but stopped yourself? A person's property is any possession — a coat, book, bike, paper, pencil, game, house, car, yard, furniture, or anything else that belongs to the person. Maybe you were angry at someone and you were tempted to get even by damaging something belonging to the person. Or perhaps you were with some friends and came close to participating in an act of vandalism because the group pressured you to "join in." Tell us what happened and what caused you to change your mind. Take a few moments to think it over. The topic is, "I Stopped Myself from Damaging Someone's Property."

Discussion Questions:

1. Why is it wrong to damage or hurt in any way another person's things?
2. Has anyone ever damaged a possession of yours? How did you feel?
3. What can you do if your friends are pressuring you to do something you know is wrong?

A Time I Helped Without Being Asked
A Sharing Circle

Objectives:
The students will:
— describe the difference between choosing to do something and being told to do it.
— state the importance of assuming responsibility for things that need to be done.

Introduce the Topic:

Today we're going to talk about taking the initiative — about accepting responsibility without being told to by an adult. Our topic is, "A Time I Helped Without Being Asked."

Think of a time when you saw something that needed to be done and took it upon yourself to do it. No one had to tell you or ask you or even hint to you that it needed doing. Maybe you walked into the kitchen one evening and saw a sink full of dirty dishes and, instead of just ignoring the mess, you cleaned it up. Or maybe you saw someone drop and spill or break something and you got down and helped pick up the pieces. Perhaps a neighbor was searching up and down the street for a missing pet and you joined in. Or you might have stayed to help a teacher straighten up a classroom after school. You can probably think of lots of times when you decided on your own to take responsibility. Tell us about one of those times. The topic is, "A Time I Helped Without Being Asked."

Discussion Questions:

1. How did you feel when you helped without being asked?
2. How would your feelings have been different if you had been asked, or even ordered, to do the same thing?
3. What does it mean to be a responsible person?
4. Why is it important for each of us to take responsibility for things that need to be done?

Responsibility Log
A Student Self-Assessment

Objectives:
The students will:
— explain what it means to be responsible.
— relate specific examples of responsible behavior.
— monitor and describe in writing their responsible and irresponsible behaviors for a prescribed period.

Materials:
two or more copies of the "Responsibility Log" for each student; whiteboard

Procedure:
Begin by discussing the meaning of the word *responsibility*. List the following components of responsibility on the board and ask the students to think of *specific* examples that might fit under each one. (Nonspecific examples are listed in the form of do's and don'ts.) Invite them to share incidents from their own experience.

Accountability
- Think before you act.
- Before you make a decision or take an action, think about how it will affect the other people involved. What will be the consequences?
- When you do something wrong or make a mistake, admit it and accept the consequences. Don't blame others or make excuses.
- Don't take credit for the achievements of others.
- Do what you should do, or have agreed to do, even if it is difficult.

Excellence
- Set a good example in everything you do.
- Do your best.
- Don't quit — keep trying.
- Make it your goal to always be proud of your performance (schoolwork, homework, projects, completed chores, athletic or other performances, etc.)

Self-control or self-restraint
- Always control yourself.
- Don't lose your temper — throw things, scream, hit others or use bad language.
- Wait your turn.
- Show courtesy and good manners.

Being a good sport
- Win and lose with grace
- Don't brag when you win or complain and make excuses when you lose.
- Take pride in how you play the game, not just whether you win.

Continue the discussion until the students understand the meaning of responsibility and many specific examples of responsible behavior have been shared. Then announce that, for the next few days, the students are going to keep logs describing actions that are clearly responsible and clearly not responsible.

Distribute the "Responsibility Log" and go over the directions with the students. Explain that the students should write down actions that they know *are* responsible (doing their best on a homework assignment and completing it on time; admitting when they forget to do a chore; congratulating the other team when they lose a game, etc.) as well as actions they feel *are not* responsible (not paying attention in class, blaming another person, procrastinating on an assignment, etc.).

Announce a date when the completed logs are due. Allow from two to five days, depending on the maturity of your students. Commend (for their responsibility) those students who complete the logs on time.

Before collecting the logs, have the students share their results in groups of four. Finally, lead a culminating class discussion.

Discussion Questions:

1. Which do you have more of, actions which are responsible or actions which are not responsible?
2. What surprised you about the results of your log?
3. How do you feel when you take a responsible action? How do you feel when your actions are not responsible?
4. In which area of responsibility do you think you need to improve?

Responsibility Log

For the next few days, pay close attention to your actions. Write down things you say and do that are clearly responsible actions. Also, write down things you say and do that you realize are not responsible actions.

Action	Responsible? Yes or No	Reactions of Others	I Learned

Learning to Set Goals
Experience Sheet and Discussion

Objectives:

The students will:
— identify behaviors that they would like to eliminate or improve.
— write goal statements and plans for achieving behavior change.

Materials:

Responsibility Logs (from the previous activity); one copy of the experience sheet, "This Is My Goal" for each student

Procedure:

Ask the students to recall the time period during which they kept a Responsibility Log. Suggest that keeping the logs probably made them more aware of their behaviors. Ask: *How many of you identified behaviors during that time that you would like to improve?*

Point out that one of the things a responsible person does is attempt to reduce or eliminate bad habits, change undesirable behaviors, and always strive to improve him/herself. This is done through setting goals, and then achieving those goals, step by step.

Return the Responsibility Logs. Give the students a couple of minutes to review them.

Announce that you want the students to choose one behavior that they would like to improve. That behavior can be one they identified through keeping their log, but it doesn't have to be. Give the students a few moments to think this over and then ask volunteers to tell the class about the behavior they have chosen to work on.

Discuss the concept of goal setting. Explain that every time the students decide on something they want to do or accomplish, they have set a goal, whether they call it that or not. The key is <u>deciding</u>. When they actually do or accomplish the thing, they have achieved their goal.

Distribute the experience sheets and briefly review the directions. While the students are completing the sheet, circulate and help them formulate goal statements.

Have the students share their completed goal statements with a partner. Ask the partners to make a pact to help each other reach their goal — with reminders, encouragement, and questions like, "How are you doing on your goal?"

Informally check to see how much time most of the students have given themselves to reach their goal. Then be sure to check with the class at regular intervals during that time, giving the students a chance to discuss their progress.

Discussion Questions:
1. What problems have you had reaching your goals?
2. How can you solve those problems?
3. Why is goal setting part of being a responsible person?
4. What can happen if you want to change a behavior but don't bother to set a goal?

This Is My Goal
Experience Sheet

A goal is like a target. It is something you aim for. The clearer your target — the better you can see it — the easier it is to hit. Also, your target has to be within *range*. If it is too far away, you don't have a very good chance of reaching it.

Think of a behavior that you would like to improve. Describe it here:

_____
_____
_____
_____

Now, turn that description into a goal. A goal should say what you are *going* to do, instead of what you are *not going* to do. In other words, make it positive! Read the examples, below.

My goal is to:
—do a good job on my homework and turn it in on time.
—peacefully eat and talk with my brother/sister at the dinner table.
—on weekdays, get my homework done before playing.
—tell the truth.
—help mom with the dishes at least twice a week, without being asked.

Write your goal here:

_____
_____

Is your goal realistic? In other words, is it something you have both the ability and the desire to accomplish? You must want your goal very much, and you must also be able to do the things required to reach it.

What steps must you take to reach your goal?

Do you have to...improve your study area? ...stick reminders on your door or mirror? ...ask someone to help you? List the steps below:

Step 1 _____

_____

_____

Step 2 _____

_____

_____

Step 3 _____

_____

_____

Step 4 _____

_____

_____

Step 5 _____

_____

_____

When do you want to reach your goal? Write a target date here:

_____

What reward will you give yourself when you have achieved your goal?

_____

_____

I Depend on You, You Depend on Me

Experience Sheet and Discussion

Objectives:
The students will:
— explain the meaning of dependability.
— describe how one person's lack of dependability affects others in typical situations.
— identify people they depend on and describe how they depend on them.
— describe one way in which they (the students) can be depended upon.

Materials:
one copy of the experience sheet, "I Depend on You — You Depend on Me" for each student; whiteboard

Procedure:

Begin by asking the students: *How do you feel when someone praises you for being dependable?* —*Have you ever heard someone say, "I'm depending on you?"*

Ask the students to explain what it means to be dependable. Facilitate discussion, exploring various meanings of the term. In the process, read the following scenarios to the students and ask the accompanying questions. Encourage the students to think of *all* the people who might be affected in each story, and *how* they would be affected (consequences).

- Sally has a lead role in the school play. Practices are on Monday and Wednesday evenings. Sally is playing with a friend one Monday afternoon and loses track of time. She misses a rehearsal.
—*Who are the people affected by Sally's absence? How are they affected?*
—*Do you think the other actors and the director will feel they can depend on Sally in the future? Why or why not?*

- Six people plan a surprise birthday party for one of their friends. They figure out a menu and everyone agrees to bring one dish. Tom is supposed to bring a decorated birthday cake from the bakery, but he forgets to order it. An hour before the party he rushes down to the supermarket and buys a ready-made cake with no decorations.
—*Who is affected and how?*
—*If you were one of Tom's friends, would you want to depend on him for future events? Why or why not?*

- Three students are working together on a project for the science fair. They are representing their whole class. On the day of the fair, two agree to come

to the auditorium early and set up the display. The third, Lila, agrees to make a chart outlining the steps in the group's experiment. Lila buys only one piece of poster board, and then puts off making the chart until late the night before. When she messes it up, she has to wait until the next morning to get more poster board and redo the chart. By the time she gets to the auditorium, the judges have already passed her group's display.
—*Who is affected and how?*
—*What could Lila have done differently?*

Distribute the experience sheets. Instruct the students to list people they can always depend on, and describe what it is they depend on them for. In addition, tell the students to describe one thing each of the people listed can depend on them (the students) to do.

Have the students share their experience sheets in groups of three to five. Lead a follow-up class discussion.

Discussion Questions:

1. At home, are you sometimes responsible for a younger brother or sister, or for a pet? What are your parents depending on you to do?
2. How do we depend on each other here in class?
3. What are some ways in which people in a community depend on each other?
4. Does being dependable mean you can never make a mistake? Explain.

I Depend on You — You Depend on Me

Experience Sheet

Responsible people are people you can depend on. They keep their promises. They do their best, even when it is hard. They do their duty to others, to the community, and to the country.

Think of people you can always depend on. Describe one thing you depend on each person to do. Then describe one thing each person can depend on *you* to do.

People I Depend On

Name	I can always depend on this person for..	This person can always depend on me for...

People I Depend On

Name	I can always depend on this person for..	This person can always depend on me for...

Framing the Blame Game
Cartooning and Discussion

Objectives:
The students will:
— describe situations involving denial of responsibility or blaming.
— explain the importance and benefits of accepting responsibility for their actions.
— creatively demonstrate the contrast between blaming and being responsible in specific situations.

Materials:
drawing paper; colored markers, pencils, or crayons; sample cartoon strips clipped from the newspaper

Procedure:
Begin by asking the students how they feel when they get blamed for something they didn't do. Listen to their responses, and then ask: *Have you ever been in a situation where a person has done something wrong or made a mistake, and you know it, but the person denies it?*

Point out that when we deny responsibility for our actions, we are in effect blaming someone else — even if we don't actually point a finger at someone and say "she did it."

Give the students several examples of blaming and elicit many more from them. Here are some possibilities:
- A child with frosting on his/her face denies having eaten a piece of cake.
- A student fails a test and says the teacher is stupid or unfair.
- A man has a car accident and blames his wife because she was talking and taking his attention away from the road.
- A person is late for work and blames the heavy traffic.
- A teenager breaks his mother's favorite vase and says that it shouldn't have been so close to the edge of the shelf.
- A batter keeps missing the ball and claims the pitcher is lousy, the sun is in his eyes, and the spectators are making him nervous.
- A child is caught shoplifting and tells her mother, "The other kids made me do it."

Announce that the students are going to make pairs of cartoon strips, one showing a blaming situation, and the other showing the same situation but with the "guilty" character accepting responsibility in the last frame.

Distribute the art materials and make available a number of sample cartoon strips. Suggest that the students illustrate a situation from their own experience, or one that was mentioned in the earlier class discussion. Stipulate that each cartoon strip should have at least three frames, showing:
1. the incident (mistake or wrongdoing)
2. the decision concerning what to do (showing fear, guilt, confusion, inner struggle, etc.)
3. blaming/denying or acceptance of responsibility

Students whose situations require additional frames should be urged to limit the number to a maximum of six.

When the cartoons are finished, post them on a bulletin board. As a class, look at and discuss each pair of cartoons, giving praise and feedback to the artist. Spread this process over several days, if necessary, facilitating discussion during each session.

Discussion Questions:

1. Why is it hard to admit when you are wrong?
2. When you make a mess, whose job is it to clean it up? Why?
3. Does anyone ever really make you do something? Explain.
4. How do we benefit by admitting our mistakes and taking responsibility?
5. What are some of the things that can happen if we don't accept responsibility?
6. What have you learned from this activity?

Variation:

Instead of making cartoons (or as an alternative for some students), allow teams to develop two skits, one dramatizing a blaming situation and the other showing the same situation with the character accepting responsibility.

Striving for Excellence

Skits, Discussion, and Song

Objectives:

The students will:
— describe times when they did their best.
— creatively demonstrate what can happen when individuals don't do their best.
— explain the costs and benefits of pursuing excellence.

Materials:

copies of the song lyrics, "Who I Am Makes a Difference;" a simple tune for the song composed in advance; piano, guitar, or other musical instrument (optional)

Procedure:

Ask the students to think of a time when they did their very best at something — absolutely the most thorough, skillful, quality job they could do at the time. Tell them that this effort could have been made toward something very big and important or something relatively small. Emphasize that what you're after is the quality of the effort, not the importance of the end product. Suggest that the effort could have been made toward the accomplishment of such things as:
- a school project
- a game or athletic event
- a single moment in an athletic event (like a particular time at bat)
- a household chore
- baking a cake or preparing a salad
- drawing a picture
- wrapping a present
- performing in a dance or music recital
- a spelling test or spelling bee

Invite several students to briefly share their incident with the class. Be sure to ask these volunteers how they felt about themselves for doing their best — and how other people felt about them. Introduce the concept of *excellence*, and talk about developing a habit of striving for excellence in every pursuit.

Write the following list on the board:

    airline pilot
    school bus driver
    ball player
    ballet dancer
    fire fighter
    doctor
    architect or builder
    baby-sitter
    chef/cook
    automobile mechanic
    movie or TV actor
    crossing guard

Have the students form groups of three or four. Announce that each group is going to develop a skit showing what can happen if one of the people listed on the board sloughs off and doesn't do his or her best.

Have each group select a recorder and choose a subject from the list (avoiding duplications). Suggest that the groups begin by describing a specific job that their subject might be doing, and then brainstorming possible consequences of the person's not doing his/her best. This process should give the groups plenty of material for a skit. Once their scenario is established, have them assign roles and rehearse.

One at a time, have the groups perform their completed skits for the entire class. After each skit, facilitate a brief discussion, focusing on the importance of doing one's best.

Conclude the activity by singing the song, *Who I Am Makes a Difference*. (See next page.) The music is available as a download from www.songsforteaching.com, or create a tune of your own prior to singing the song. Divide the class in half (groups 1 and 2). Play or hum the tune a couple of times. Then lead group 1 in singing the first chorus (A), pointing to group 2 when they sing the words, "and the same is true for you." Lead group 2 in singing the second chorus (B), with the students pointing back at group 1 on the last line. Have the entire class sing the last chorus (C) together. Finally, repeat the first chorus, signaling the children to point at *each other* as they speak the last line loudly and firmly.

Discussion Questions:
1. Who benefits when we do our best?
2. How do you know when you are doing your best?
3. What does it cost to do your best? What, if anything, do you have to give up?
4. Does striving for excellence build good character? How?

Who I Am Makes a Difference

A.
Who I am makes a difference,
What I do makes a difference,
What I say makes a difference, each and every day.
Who I am makes a difference,
What I do makes a difference,
What I say makes a difference, and the same is true for you.

B.
Who you are makes a difference,
What you do makes a difference,
What you say makes a difference, each and every day.
Who you are makes a difference,
What you do makes a difference,
What you say makes a difference, and the same is true for us.

C.
Who we are makes a difference,
What we do makes a difference,
What we say makes a difference, each and every day.
Who we are makes a difference,
What we do makes a difference
What we say makes a difference,
Yes, I know it's true.

Repeat verse A, and repeat last line, speaking the words.

Music is available, as a download, from www.songsforteaching.com

Words and music copyright 1996 by Linda K. Williams

Self-Control

Story:

An Alterna-Tive Tale
Experience Sheet

Sharing Circles:

I Wanted It Now, But I Waited Till Later
A Time I Felt Anger and Handled It Well

Activities:

A Wave of Self-Control
Game And Discussion

In My Control
Experiments in External vs. Internal Control

Control Yourself
Discussion and Informal Self-Assessment

Taking Control of Anger
Experience Sheet and Discussion

Song:

If You're Angry and You Know It

An Alterna-Tive Tale
by Dianne Schilling

The Want family lived in a big, sturdy house with a yard the size of a small park on a quiet street in the town of Amity.

It was a good thing that the house was big, because fully sixteen Wants ranging in age from eighteen months to 73 years lived within its walls. It was an even better thing that the walls were thick and sturdy, because the Wants tended to be — well, *loud* probably says it best. And it was indeed fortunate that the yard was deep enough to keep the house well back from the quiet street — or it would not have been quiet at all.

The reason for all the noise in the Want house can be summed up in one word — *confusion*. It wasn't that the Wants didn't love one another — they did. But they were active, independent people and it seemed as though every Want always wanted something different from every other Want.

For example, at around seven o'clock each weekday morning, approximately thirteen hungry, hurrying Wants would arrive in the kitchen eager for breakfast. These were the family members who needed to leave for work or school. They were always rushed and often irritable. If four of them wanted eggs, you could be sure that only one preferred scrambled, while the other three insisted on fried, poached, and boiled. Assuming they were lucky enough to find four pans and fit them on the four burners of the stove, this left no room for the Wants who hurried in wanting to fix oatmeal, french toast, pancakes, or to boil water for tea.

At nine o'clock at night, cries went up for more different TV shows than there were channels to choose from. And on Saturday morning, at least nine or ten Wants would claim to need one of the family's two cars for errands or activities that had absolutely no relation in time or location to one another.

The only time two Wants ever wanted the same thing was when there was only one of it. For instance, Wilbur and Winnifred could always be counted on to want the washing machine at the same hour of the same day. And if there was only one light bulb left, at least five desktop or bedside reading lamps would blow out at virtually the same instant. You can probably imagine how it was in the Want house. Arguments, yelling, endless discussions, and very few decisions. Rarely could people agree on who should go to the store and buy the groceries. Or what groceries ought to be bought. Or how they ought to be prepared. There were always sixteen different ideas about where the Christmas tree should be placed, and eleven volunteers who wanted to put the angel on the top of the tree.

Visiting home from college one weekend, Wanda Want (who was studying business management) said, "What this family needs most is a household manager.

Maybe then some decisions would get made."

This suggestion was followed by a loud and lively discussion among several members of the family. Everyone had a slightly different viewpoint, and everyone expressed it. Of course, no agreements were reached so no decisions were made. Wiley and Wilomena went off to the kitchen table and tried to write a want ad — together. They argued about it for hours. They couldn't agree on what a household manager should do. They couldn't even decide how many lines to write, or where to place the ad, or when to stop arguing and eat lunch.

Finally, Wanda wrote the ad herself. She was smart enough not to ask for anyone else's ideas or reactions. But when it appeared in the newspaper, she cut it out and posted it on the front of the refrigerator for everyone to see:

Full-time Household Manager wanted for very large, active family. Cooking and cleaning not required. Must know how to promote self-control, conflict resolution, and decision making. Call 756-8742 weekdays after 7:00 p.m. and ask for Wanda.

The phone number was for Wanda's college dormitory. For the next two weeks, Wanda conducted interviews during the week. When she came home on the first Friday night, she refused to discuss the progress of her plan with any member of the family. But when she came home at the end of the second week, Wanda made an announcement. She said, "Tomorrow morning at 10:00 a.m., the Want Family Household Manager will arrive for her first day of work. I would like all of you to be present." Then, without another word, she climbed the stairs to her room.

On Saturday morning at exactly 10:00 a.m., the doorbell rang. For one glorious moment, every activity, every discussion, and every argument stopped. The Want house was silent.

Then it exploded. Dishes and pans clattered into the sink, chair legs scraped across the floor and doors in every corner of the house swung open and slammed shut. The sound of running, walking and scuffling footsteps mixed with whispered chatter, yelling and laughter as everyone hurried to the door.

A collision was inevitable. Weld and Wendy slid into the entryway and dove for the door as if it were first base at a Little League game. William dove for the door from halfway up the entry staircase, and Winter careened down the hall on her skateboard. There was a loud crash. The front door shuddered and rattled on its hinges — then burst open to reveal four young Wants in a heap on the floor surrounded by a curious (and curious-looking) crowd of twelve onlookers.

Leaning against the porch railing was a tall, angular woman with black hair and knowing dark eyes. Her arms were folded loosely across the front of a bright yellow warm-up suit. A smile of amusement played at one corner of her broad mouth. Leaning on its end against the railing next to the women was a long leather carrying case that almost equaled her in height.

The woman watched with interest as Weld, Wendy, William and Winter untangled themselves. Then she picked up her carrying case and stepped through the door without being asked. Breaking a path across the entryway, the woman walked briskly to the living room and stopped.

"My name is Alterna," she said, pivoting smoothly to survey her audience. "Alterna Tive." Alterna looked steadily into sixteen pairs of eyes — one pair at a time. A grin traveled back and forth between her large ears. "Rhymes with jive," she added in an exaggerated drawl.

Everyone stared, speechless. Then Wanda stepped forward. "Welcome Alterna," she said, extending her hand. "Allow me to introduce my family." Wanda moved down the line and Alterna followed her, shaking hands and repeating each person's name. "Weston, Wisteria, Wooley, Walter..."

When the introductions were over, Alterna stepped back and asked cheerfully, "Well, what's everybody doing today?"

"Shopping!"

"Homework!"

"Little League!"

"The lake!"

"Weston can't go fishing 'til he mows the lawn," said Winter, loudly.

"It's not my turn," yelled Weston. "It's yours, and you know it!"

"I did it last week."

"Well, somebody else will have to do it then, because I get stuck with that job all the time," Weston said firmly.

Alterna was unzipping her carrying case. She reached in and lifted out a leggy metal contraption and, with a few pulls and snaps, transformed it into an easel. Then she unrolled a pad of paper and hung it from the top of the easel. A fat, black pen appeared in her hand.

"It's a big yard," observed Alterna, holding up her hand to quiet the group. "I bet that when you do the yard work, it takes you all day."

Nodding heads — and groans.

"If you've done yard work even once during the last year, come up here and sign your name," said Alterna, tossing her pen to Weston.

Two minutes later, the chart had nine names on it.

"Hey, look what you just did," exclaimed Alterna. "There was only one pen and you took turns using it. And I didn't even have to tell you to!"

Shrugs and giggles.

Alterna studied the list. "So, this is the yard team," she said. "Is there anyone else who would like to be on the yard team?"

Seven-year-old Woody stepped forward. "Me," he announced. Alterna gave him the pen and he signed his name.

"Let's see," said Alterna, "we have one big yard, and one big team with ten individual members. How many ways can a team of ten make sure that the yard gets cleaned every week?"

"Take turns."

"Make a schedule."

"Do it together."

"Divide up the work."

"Divide up the yard."

"Have two teams of five, and appoint judges to decide which team did the best work."

"Or the fastest!"

"And award a prize!"

Alterna was writing all the ideas down on a clean sheet of paper. "Tell you what," she smiled. "I think the team has some terrific ideas. And I think the team can find a solution to the problem without the rest of us hanging around. Weston, since you seem to have the most yard experience, you're in charge of this meeting. Here's the pen — and here are the rules."

Alterna looked from one team member to another. "Only one person talks at a time. Everybody else listens. Keep listing ideas until you run out of them. Then use the ideas to create a solution. The solution doesn't have to be perfect, but it has to be one that every member of the team will agree to try for at least two weeks. No exceptions. Okay? We'll check back with you later."

Alterna went with the rest of the family into the kitchen. "I could sure use a cup of tea," she said. "Do you have any?"

"I'll fix it," offered Wayne.

"No, let me do it," begged Wilomena.

They began to struggle over the tea kettle.

"Hold it!" cried Alterna. "Let me have the kettle for a second."

Alterna shook the tea kettle to make certain it was empty and then placed it on the floor and gave it a spin. "When it stops, the person closest to where the spout is pointing gets to make the tea. And since I drink a lot of tea, the other person gets to make it next time."

Wayne won the spin. He fixed spicy orange tea for everyone.

Throughout the day, Alterna Tive migrated from one part of the house to another, watching the Wants closely, and jumping in whenever an argument erupted, which of course was often. When a conflict was complicated, Alterna used her easel. Most of the time, she just used her head.

"Turn the stereo off, Warren. I'll never finish this report if I can't concentrate," complained Wanda from her seat at the computer.

"Wanda, just because you're a big college student doesn't mean you can take over the living room every weekend. I was here first."

"Warren, I'm not taking over anything. I just want some quiet. You can play your music anytime, but I have to finish this report before Monday."

"I cannot play my music anytime. I go to school too, remember?"

"Oh," said Wanda tartly. "Then maybe you should be doing your homework."

"Hey, contestants," cried Alterna. "Cool it. Put your lip power to rest and use your brainpower to figure out how both of you can win. Does the computer move?"

"We never move it, but I suppose we could," replied Wanda.

"Well..." hummed Alterna, her eyes fixed on Warren.

"Gotcha!" said Warren, jumping up from the sofa. "Come on, big sister. I'll help you carry the hardware to your haven upstairs."

"Where do you think you're going with those car keys," demanded Wilbur. He was chasing Wysteria down the hall.

"I have to pick up Wendy and Weld from Little League practice," called Wysteria over her shoulder. She quickened her pace.

"You don't have to leave yet. The practice isn't over for another hour," shouted Wilbur. "I was just about to run over to the building-supply store."

"There's a sale on sheets at the department store. I have to stop there first."

Wysteria was out the door, with Wilbur in hot pursuit. "I won't be able to fix the screen door today," insisted Wilbur.

"Wilbur, I have to go now because this is the last day of the sale. Why can't you just wait till I get back."

"Because it will be too late," shouted Wilbur in reply. "I have to fix the screen before dark."

Wysteria lifted the garage door. "No you don't. It's been broken for a month. Another day won't hurt."

"I don't want to wait another day! I want to do it today!"

The battle was broken by the blare of the car horn. When she had captured their attention, Alterna pulled her arm from the driver's window of the car and stepped out of the garage. "My goodness," she scolded.

"Two smart people putting all their energy into fighting over one car. Why don't you put your energy into finding a way to share the car and accomplish all three errands — the sheets, the building supplies, and the Little League pick up."

Wilbur stared at the ground and grumbled. Wysteria looked embarrassed. "Maybe you could pick up the kids," she said. "After you get your supplies." Wysteria offered Wilbur the car keys.

"Yeah, I could do that, but then you'd miss the sheet sale."

"No," said Wysteria. "I could go after you get back."

"Or I could drop you off at the department store first, and pick you up after I pick up Weld and Wendy," suggested Wilbur.

"That might be better," said Wysteria. "Come on. Let's not waste any more time."

Alterna stayed for dinner. Between the pasta and the pie, she made an announcement. "Before I leave tonight," she said. "I am going to appoint two people to be systems managers for the next week. My experience has taught me that a lot of conflicts can be avoided if you take the time to set things up right from the beginning. For example, a systems manager might design a car-use schedule and post it near the door. People who wanted to use one of the cars would sign for it in advance. Another thing a systems manager might do is notice when the family is running out of something that everybody uses — like shampoo or bananas — and put that item on the shopping list. As a systems manager, your job is to pay attention to the kinds of conflicts people have, and then try to figure out ways of preventing them."

All but two Wants immediately applied for the position of systems manager. "I have fourteen applicants for two jobs," said Alterna. She paused for several seconds and then asked matter-of-factly, "Who would be willing to withdraw his or her application and wait till another week?"

Three Wants withdrew.

"That leaves eleven applicants for two jobs," said Alterna patiently. "You know, if they want to, systems managers can ask for advice and suggestions. Maybe some of you would be willing to serve as advisors this week — if you're asked to that is."

Seven more Wants withdrew their applications.

"That leaves four applicants for two jobs," said Alterna. "I need two more withdrawals."

"Wait a minute," chimed in Walter. "Who says that a job has to be for just one person? Why can't each job be filled by a team of two?"

A chorus of approval sounded from around the dining table. Alterna grinned and gestured her thumbs-up approval. "Now you're really getting the idea!" she laughed.

"Alterna," asked little Wooley. "Are you coming back every Saturday?"

"I think two or three more Saturdays will be enough," replied Alterna. "After that, you won't need me anymore. In my business," smiled Alterna broadly, "short-term employment is a sign of success."

Discussion Questions:

1. What are some examples of self-control that you heard in this story? When did the characters show a lack of self-control?
2. Why is it important for only one person to talk at a time when you are trying to solve a problem?
3. Why did Alterna tell the yard team that its solution for doing yard work didn't have to be perfect?
4. Spinning the kettle on the floor was a game of chance. What are some other games of chance that can be used to settle conflicts?
5. How can we keep from getting locked into seeing just one solution — our own?
6. If Warren and Wanda hadn't been able to move the computer, what else could they have done?
7. Why do you think Wysteria was embarrassed when Alterna found her and Wilbur fighting over the car?
8. What did Alterna do to help the 14 applicants avoid a conflict over the systems manager job?

An Alterna-Tive Tale
Experience Sheet

What did you learn about self-control from the story of the Want family? What did you learn about solving conflicts? Think about the story as you answer these questions:

1. Have you ever been in a situation where everyone was "out of control?" What was going on and what did each person do?

   _____
   _____
   _____

2. Think of a conflict you had with someone during the last week. Are there ways that conflict could have been prevented? if so, how? If not, why?

   _____
   _____
   _____

3. What did Alterna mean when she said that in her business, short term employment is a sign of success?

   _____
   _____

4. Alterna Tive got her name from the word alternative. It's a perfect name for her. Can you explain why?

   _____
   _____
   _____

I Wanted It Now, But I Waited Till Later

A Sharing Circle

Objectives:

The students will:
—define self-control and discuss how it develops.
—give and receive credit for times when they exerted self-control.

Introduce the Topic:

Our circle today is about controlling feelings. We're going to talk about having a strong need or desire for something, but being able to put off having or doing it until a more appropriate time. Our topic is, "I Wanted It Now, But I Waited Till Later."

Think of a time when you controlled your feelings and tell us about the experience. Maybe it was something really simple, like craving a candy bar a few minutes before dinner, but waiting until after dinner to eat it. Or perhaps you wanted to turn on the TV or some music when you got home from school, but made yourself do your homework first. Have you ever wanted to phone and tell a friend something but realized it was a little too late in the evening and instead waited until the next day? That can be pretty hard to do. Have you ever forced yourself to stay inside to talk with visiting relatives when you wanted to be outside playing with your friends? That can be tough, too. Describe what happened and tell us how you managed to control yourself. The topic is, "I Wanted It Now, But I Waited Till Later."

Discussion Questions:

1. What does it mean to have self-control?
2. Do babies have self-control? How do we develop self-control?
3. What would families and classrooms be like if no one showed any self-control?
4. How do you feel about yourself when you succeed in having self-control?

A Time I Felt Anger and Handled It Well

A Circle Session

Objectives:

The students will:
—verbally acknowledge themselves and others for successfully controlling anger.
—identify techniques for controlling anger.

Introduce the Topic:

Anger is one of the hardest emotions to deal with. It doesn't feel good and it's hard to control. In this session, we're going to talk about successfully controlling anger. Our topic is, "A Time I Felt Anger and Handled It Well."

Think of a time when you were angry at something or someone, but you bit your lip, or counted to ten, or did something else to keep from blowing up. You may have been mad at a friend, parent, teacher, brother or sister, and it could have been over something important or a tiny thing. Tell us what happened and what you did to control yourself, but please don't mention any names. The topic is, "A Time I Felt Anger and Handled It Well."

Discussion Questions:

1. Why is it important to control anger? What kinds of things can anger lead to if it isn't controlled?
2. What are some ways to let anger out, like air from a balloon, without actually getting angry?
3. What have you learned about anger from this session?

A Wave of Self-Control

Game and Discussion

Objectives:
The students will:
— spontaneously complete sentences related to self-control
— identify do's and don'ts related to self-control.
— describe how having specific behavioral goals can lead to greater self-control.

Materials:
whiteboard or chart paper

Procedure:
If possible, have the students sit in one large circle. Pick a sentence starter from the list. "Send" the starter quickly around the circle like a wave. (If the students are sitting in rows, send the wave down one row and up the next.) Have each student in turn rise, tack an ending on the sentence, and sit back down. At times you might want to send the same starter around two or three times. Or begin a second starter immediately after the first one passes the last person in the group.

Sentence Starters
- When I'm angry at someone, I usually...
- A good way to control my temper is to...
- A rule I have trouble following is...
- Self-control is important because...
- I sometimes get in trouble for...
- I get impatient about...
- I don't like waiting for...
- I'm getting better about controlling...
- When I feel impatient, I...
- A good way to blow off steam is...

After the game, point out that all of the sentence starters had to do with self-control. (Or ask the students to guess the central theme.)

Explain that having self-control is part of being a responsible person. If you have self-control, you are able to *restrain* and *regulate* your own behavior. Ask the students to name some *do's* and *don'ts* associated with self-control. Write their suggestions on the board, creating lists that contain items like these:

DO:
raise your hand
wait your turn
sit quietly
be polite
have consideration
be patient
show respect for others
be understanding

DON'T:
fidget
interrupt
lose your temper
throw things
scream
hit others
use bad language.

Next, ask the students how they might go about changing their behavior and gaining more self-control. Listen to their suggestions, and write these steps on the board:

1. Decide exactly what behavior you want to change.
2. Set a self-control goal.
3. Think of things you can do, or not do, to help yourself reach your goal.
4. Keep working on the new behavior, little by little, until it becomes a habit.

Give the students an example like this one:

Rick had a hard time keeping his room clean. He set a goal to develop the habit of picking up his things every morning before school and every evening at bedtime. Since he shared the room with his younger brother, Mike, Rick had to enlist Mike's cooperation. He decided to organize the closet and the shelves so that his books, toys, and other gear were kept separate from Mike's. When Mike left things lyng around, Rick would ask nicely, "Please pick that up — I'm working on my goal." Each day he spent a little time doing the tasks that needed to be done, and eventually his parents no longer had to scold him about keeping his room clean. He had achieved his goal!

Conclude the activity with further discussion.

Discussion Questions:

1. How much self-control do babies have?
2. Do you think people gain more self-control as they grow up? Why or why not?
3. Is gaining self-control as you get older automatic, or do you have to work at it? Explain.
4. Over what behavior would you like to have more control?

Extension:

Use this activity as a springboard to helping individual students set self-control goals. Work through the goal-setting and planning process with these students on a one-to-one basis. With younger students, draw and duplicate a picture of a target on 8.5 x 11 paper. Within the target make a number of concentric circles. Every day that a student shows progress toward his or her individual self-control goal (which should be written on the sheet), allow the student to color in one of the circles, starting with the outside edge of the target and working toward the center. Use many different colors. When the entire target is filled in, congratulate the student for reaching his or her goal.

In My Control

Experiments in External vs. Internal Control

Objectives:
The students will:
— experience the difference between control by others and self-control.
— explain how, in growing up, greater self-control earns greater freedom.

Materials:
none

Procedure:

Announce that the students are going to participate in several short games or experiments in order to experience different types and degrees of control as well as freedom from control.

Instruct the students to listen carefully and follow your directions. Then, in your own words, say:

You are computer-controlled robots and I am your master, giving you computer commands. You can only do what I say and nothing else. Your body movements are mechanical and slow.

Give the students 3 minutes of robot commands, e.g., "Stand up!" "Walk two steps to your right!" "Shake hands with the person closest to you!" "Raise your right arm!"

For the next few minutes you are free to do anything you want. However, first you must lock arms with three other people and keep your arms locked.

Give the students 3 minutes. Then say, "Freeze!"

Unlock your arms, and for the next few minutes you may do anything you want, as long as you don't hurt anyone else or leave the room.

Give the students 3 minutes. Then say, "Freeze!"

You are robots again. Stand very straight and very still. There is a fly on your nose but you cannot move any part of your body without my command. Pretend the fly is really there and it tickles. Really act it out.

Give the students 2 minutes. Then say, "Okay, brush it off. Freeze!"

Pick a partner. One of you is now the computer master and the other is the robot. Masters, you may give your robot any commands you like, as long as they are safe. Robots, you must follow the commands.

After 2 minutes, say, "Switch!"

Conclude the activity with a discussion about different types and levels of control.

Discussion Questions:

1. How did it feel to be in someone else's control?
2. When you had freedom, how much self-control did you exercise?
3. Have you ever felt like a robot or a slave? What was that like?
4. As children grow up, they are usually given a little more freedom each year; however, to get it they are expected to show a little more self-control. What would happen if they were given complete freedom before they developed self-control?

Control Yourself
Discussion and Informal Self-Assessment

Objectives:
The students will:
—describe examples of self-control and self-management.
—demonstrate behaviors associated with self-control
—affirm themselves for their own levels of self-control.

Materials:
whiteboard

Procedure:

Begin this session by asking the students what the term *self-control* means. Listen to and reflect the students' responses. In the process, establish that having self-control means being able to *restrain* and regulate one's own behavior. It means not losing your temper, not throwing things, not screaming, hitting others, or using bad language. Then say: *Think of a time when your emotions were so strong that you couldn't control yourself. Maybe you didn't want to cry or yell or laugh, but the feelings were overpowering.*

Invite volunteers to tell the class about their experiences. Ask one or two to act out their incidents, demonstrating exactly what happened.

Next, whisper one of the following situations to a volunteer and have that student act out the situation in pantomime (nonverbally). Have the class guess what is happening and identify the emotion that the student is trying to control.

—*You just crashed your bike, banging your leg badly, in front of several older kids.*
—*You get back a paper that you worked very hard on. It's covered with red marks and graded C-.*
—*Walking home at dusk, you turn a corner and practically run right into a big skunk.*
—*While your teacher is explaining an assignment, you see another student do something hysterically funny and try to keep from breaking up.*
—*Your parent restricts you for something your brother or sister did.*
—*You are walking home alone after just learning that a boy or girl you have a crush on likes you, too.*

Repeat this process with the remainder of the situations and a new volunteer each time. After each pantomime, talk about methods typically used to control reactions to various emotions (biting tongue, clenching fists, taking deep breaths, blinking, stiffening muscles, looking away, etc.)

Draw a long horizontal line across the board. At one end write, "Volcanic Vicki." At the other end write, "Restrained Robert." Explain to the students that the line is a self-control *continuum* and that Vicki and Robert represent the extreme endpoints. Ask the students to help you describe Vicki and Robert. Have fun with this and encourage the students to exaggerate their descriptions. For example:

Volcanic Vicki is going off all the time. At the slightest provocation, steam spews from her nostrils, tears from her eyes, and agonizing, earth shaking sounds from her throat. Vicki was once able to control herself for 20 seconds, and that was when a bee landed on her nose.

Restrained Robert looks a little like an automated store mannequin. His expression almost never changes and his movements are stiff and controlled. People have exhausted themselves trying to make Robert laugh, or blink, or get angry. But Robert would rather die than lose control.

Ask two or three students at a time to write their names somewhere on the continuum. Explain that before they do this, they must decide how much self-control they have. Are they closer to Vicki's end of the continuum or Robert's? Give all of the students an opportunity to place themselves on the line.

Lead a culminating class discussion, focusing on the concepts of self-control and self-management. Then, with the last few minutes remaining, play a little game with the students. Tell them to sit absolutely still, without fidgeting, talking, or blinking. Explain that the last student to move is the winner. Time the students and proclaim the winner, "Self-control King" or "Self-control Queen" for the day.

Discussion Questions:

1. Why is it important to learn self-control?
2. What would school be like if students and teachers never made any effort to manage their feelings or behavior?
3. What does self-management have to do with responsibility?
4. What do your parents mean when they tell you to "be on your best behavior?"
5. How do you feel when you successfully control yourself?

Variation:

With younger students, draw an imaginary self-control line on the floor and have the children stand in the spot that represents their place on the continuum. Have two students act out the parts of Volcanic Vicki and Restrained Robert while standing at either end of the imaginary line.

Taking Control of Anger
Experience Sheet and Discussion

Objectives:
The students will:
— understand that anger is normal.
— state that they can learn to control their reactions to anger.
— observe and evaluate their own behaviors in anger-provoking situations.

Materials:
one copy of the experience sheet, "Chart Your Anger," for each student; whiteboard

Note:
Contrary to popular myth, "letting off steam", and "getting your anger out" are not the ways to manage angry feelings. They actually make people angrier. Anger is self-reinforcing; therefore, helping kids learn to dissipate anger through positive, pro-social thoughts and actions is far more beneficial and the purpose of this activity.

Procedure:
Begin by telling the students a real story about a recent time when you got angry. For example, you might say:

I hope you don't mind if I share this with you. I was waiting in a line of cars to get on the freeway this morning and this person zoomed by me on the shoulder of the on ramp. He was driving so fast, it looked like he was going to lose control of his car. He passed up all of us who were waiting patiently for our turn. I was really angry and upset by this.

Ask the students if they ever get angry. Talk a little about the kinds of things that provoke anger in them.

Ask the students to take out a sheet of paper (or distribute paper) and write a list of events or situations that make them angry. Give the students 5 or 10 minutes to do this. When they have finished, tell them to go back through their list and number the items from "Most Angry" (#1) to "Least Angry" (highest number).

Next, return to your earlier story, and talk about your behaviors when you were angry. Continuing with the previous example, you might say:

When I was angry with that driver this morning, I was tempted to start yelling, but I knew that yelling would just keep me focused on my anger. Doing that would only reinforce my angry feelings. The woman in front of me laid on her horn, and I heard a couple of other horns blaring, too.

Explain that you and the other people all felt angry. Point out that some ways of managing anger are more effective than others. In your own words tell the students, *The other drivers expressed their anger outwardly by honking their horns and probably yelling and doing other things. What I did was a little different. Yelling, honking my horn, and focusing on my anger wasn't going to make me feel better. Rather, what I wanted to do was to let my anger dissipate by maintaining self-control. Perhaps the other driver was having an emergency. Maybe he was just being rude. I couldn't do anything about his behavior, but I could maintain my self control and not drive myself into more anger, or stay in that angry place.*

Give the students an opportunity to talk about ways in which they express anger.

Then, have the students turn their sheet of paper over and, on the back, list things they do when they are angry. Give them another 5 to 10 minutes to complete this second list. When they have finished, tell them to go back through the list and number the items from those that reflect the "Most Self Control" (#1) to "Least Effective" (highest number).

Ask volunteers to share their lists with the class. Discuss the effects of various reactions to anger, and the relative amounts of self-control they require.

Distribute the experience sheets. Go over the directions, and answer any questions about use of the chart. Explain that the students are to chart their reactions to anger for one week. Give the students an exact due date.

When the charts are completed, have the students discuss them in small groups. Suggest that they take turns sharing one or two events from their chart, and talk about which behaviors worked for them, and which didn't.

Conclude the activity with a class discussion. Spend time talking about ways to learn and practice high self-control behaviors. Another excellent way to conclude this activity is by leading the students in the song "If You're Angry and You Know It."

Discussion Questions:

1. What similarities did you notice in the things that made us angry?
2. What were the most common reactions?
3. What are the benefits of being in control?
4. What are the dangers of reacting with low self-control?
5. What high self-control behavior would you like to learn? How can you go about learning it?

Chart your Anger!
Experience Sheet

Getting angry is a reaction that comes naturally. You hardly ever have to think about it. Here's what you do have to think about: How to control yourself when you are angry. That's much harder. That takes work, but in the end it's better for you and everyone else.

Use the chart for one week. Every time you get angry, write it down. In the EVENT column, describe what happened to make you angry. In the REACTION column, put the number of the reaction that comes closest to what you did. Choose from the list at the bottom of the page. If you did two or more things, put two or more numbers. At the end of the week, answer the questions below. Then, bring your experience sheet back to class.

Answer these questions *after* you have completed your chart:

1. Were any of the things that made you angry preventable? _____ How?

_____
_____
_____
_____
_____

2. Which high self-control actions work best for you?

_____
_____
_____

3. Which high self-control actions would you like to learn?

_____
_____
_____

EVENT	REACTION

Reactions
LOW SELF-CONTROL

1. Physically hurt someone.
2. Damage or destroy property.
3. Use alcohol or drugs to forget about it.
4. Yell accusations or threats.
5. Call a person lots of bad names.
6. Try to get someone in trouble by telling.
7. Punch a pillow or a punching bag.
8. Ignore it and pretend nothing happened.
9. Take several deep breaths.
10. Count to ten.
11. Assertively say what you think.
12. Go for a bike ride, or play a sport or game.
13. Listen to music.
14. Take a walk, run, or swim.
15. Do a relaxation exercise or meditation.
16. Write about it in your diary or journal.
17. Share your feelings with someone you trust.
18. Try to understand what is going on for the other person.

HIGH SELF-CONTROL

If You're Angry and You Know It

If you're angry and you know it, talk it over, (I'm angry!)
If you're angry and you know it, talk it over, (I'm angry!)
If you're angry and you know it, that's okay, you can control it!
If you're angry and you know it, talk it over, (I'm angry!)

(2)
If you're angry and you know it, count to ten, (One, two, three...)
If you're angry and you know it, count to ten, (One, two, three...)
If you're angry and you know it, that's okay, you can control it!
If you're angry and you know it, count to ten, (One, two, three...)

(3)
If you're angry and you know it, stop and think, (Hm-m-m!)
If you're angry and you know it, stop and think, (Hm-m-m!)
If you're angry and you know it, that's okay, you can control it!
If you're angry and you know it, stop and think, (Hm-m-m!)

(4)
If you're angry and you know it, pound a pillow, (Whap, whap!)
If you're angry and you know it, pound a pillow, (Whap, whap!)
If you're angry and you know it, that's okay, you can control it!
If you're angry and you know it, pound a pillow, (Whap, whap!)

(5)
If you're angry and you know it, take a walk, (Walk, walk!)
If you're angry and you know it, take a walk, (Walk, walk!)
If you're angry and you know it, that's okay, you can control it!
If you're angry and you know it, take a walk, (Walk, walk!)

(6)
If you're angry and you know it, just relax, (Ah-h-h!)
If you're angry and you know it, just relax, (Ah-h-h!)
If you're angry and you know it, that's okay, you can control it!
If you're angry and you know it, just relax, (Ah-h-h!)

Tune: popular children's folk song, "If You're Happy and You Know It, Clap Your Hands."

Music is available, as a download, from www.songsforteaching.com

Lyrics copyright 1996 by Linda K. Williams

Peer Pressure

Story:

Sweet Revenge
Experience Sheet

Sharing Circles:

A Time I Said No
What's Good and Bad About Peer Pressure

Activities:

Identifying Sources of Influence
Experience Sheet and Discussion

Feel the Difference
Assertiveness Practice

Dozens of Ways to Say No
Brainstorming, Role Play and Discussion

No! X 4 = Goodbye!
Discussion and Skill Practice

Song:

I Can Say "No!" When I Want To

Sweet Revenge
by Tom Pettepiece

"Dare you!" Morey said.

I gulped. Morey had dared me before to do things at school, like ten pull-ups on the high bar, or kick the girl's ball during recess. Once he even dared me to stick out my tongue at the teacher while she wasn't looking, which I did, though I could have sworn she saw me at the last minute when she turned her head and I yanked my tongue quickly into hiding.

Truth is, I was weary of Morey's dares, and today's felt worse than ever before. My stomach gurgled like an empty cavern. My legs felt rubbery — I wobbled like a Saturday morning cartoon character.

I was standing with Morey and three other boys right below Mr. Brickle's big picture window, where Mr. Brickle stood every day after school and watched us kids walk home. If he saw anyone goofing off, or bothering the girls, or — worst of all — stepping on his property in the slightest, on any part, the grass or the flower bed with tulip bulbs waiting for Spring, he'd pound on the window and shake his fist at us. And if that didn't work, he'd disappear from view for a moment, then reappear on the porch shouting, "You kids better stay out of my yard if you know what's good for you!" None of us ever really knew what wouldn't be good for us if we didn't, but we never had the courage to defy the old man and find out. Until now that is.

All eyes were on me, the growing silence giving away my cowardice in the face of pressure. I didn't know which was worse, the fear of Brickle or the fear of saying no to my friends.

"Come on, James," one of the guys urged. "Are you or aren't you?"

"Yeah. You're the one who's always talking so tough, saying 'Mr. Brickle is as dumb as a pickle,' and stuff like that. Are you going to throw that rock or not?"

I admit, I'd wanted to get even for a long time — ever since Brickle yelled at me for parking my bike on the sidewalk in front of his house while I ran after my dog. When I came back the bike was gone, and I didn't get it back for a week. My parents made me go over and apologize to Mr. Brickle, even though they agreed that I hadn't done anything wrong. The sidewalk *was* public property. Only problem was, Mr. Brickle or someone else walking by might have fallen trying to go around the bike blocking their way.

That same night after dinner, my buddies and I had met on the corner of Mr. Brickle's street and talked about getting even with the old man by breaking his precious picture window. Then he couldn't stand there and stare at us anymore. Morey was convinced that tonight was the perfect time, since on our way home from school we'd seen Mr. Brickle's son drive off with him. It was twilight, dark enough so we couldn't be seen from the street in the bushes beneath the window, but light enough for Morey to find the medium-sized rock he now held out to me.

"You're chicken, James," one of the guys said. "All talk and no action," said another. "You've got a yellow streak down your back longer than the highway," Morey blurted out.

"Well, you do it then, Big Mouth," I shot back.

"He didn't take *my* bike, man."

"Yeah, but he's yelled at you as much as me, calling you a punk kid and a juvenile delinquent."

The other boys murmured agreement. It was true. Brickle had insulted us all at one time or another. Not one kid who walked by his house had been spared the wrath of his cruel words. Hadn't Mr. Brickle ever been a kid? What was wrong with him anyway?

"Well, James?" they all echoed in unison. "It's getting dark. Let's go. Now or never."

"Okay, okay." I was starting to feel annoyed at the pressure. I figured they were just as scared as I was, that's why they were trying to goad me into doing it. Breaking someone's window was wrong — even the window of a mean old man like Brickle.

I decided to fake them out. "I'll do it on one condition," I said.

"What?" asked Morey.

"That we're all in this together. If anyone gets caught, we all get caught. And if anyone runs, the deal is off. Got it?"

They all looked at each other for a moment, then back at me.

"Okay. Do it."

I stepped back so I could see the front of the house, dominated by the window. It was an old wooden house, built over sixty years ago, with brick around the bottom. The section with the big window jutted out toward the street, so while it provided a perfect viewing stand for Mr. Brickle, it also made a perfect target.

I tossed the rock up and down in my palm, higher each time. I eyed the glass as though it were a bull's-eye on a shooting range. "Let's get Brickle, let's get Brickle," I began to chant. My arm was up in the air now, making circles as if I was preparing to throw the rock all the way to China. "Get Brickle, get Brickle, get Brickle."

"Quiet!" hissed Morey. "You want everyone in the neighborhood to hear you?"

Ignoring Morey's warning, I shouted, "Spread out guys, so you don't get hit by flying glass! Here I go... one, two..."

"RUN!" cried Morey as they all scattered like squirrels fleeing the hunter.

"Three!"

I held onto the rock for a moment before letting it drop harmlessly to the ground. I turned away just in time to see the other guys disappear around a corner.

Heading home, I noticed that the wobbliness in my legs was gone. I started to whistle a tune. "What'll Morey come up with next?" I wondered.

Discussion Questions:

1. What was the conflict James felt before he made his decision?
2. Did the fact that Mr. Brickle was a mean person make it all right to destroy his property? Why not?
3. Why didn't Morey throw the rock himself?
4. How else could the boys have handled their anger at Mr. Brickle?
5. Did James really want to break the window? How do you know?
6. What did the boys say and do to try to pressure James into throwing the rock?
7. What was James trying to accomplish by "faking out" Morey and the other boys?
8. What are some other ways that James could have resisted the pressure of his friends?
9. How do you think James felt as he headed home?

Sweet Revenge
Experience Sheet

Think about the story of James and his friends. The other boys tried to pressure James into throwing the rock through Mr. Bickle's window. James acted like he was going along with them for a while, but he was always in control. James knew from the beginning that he wasn't going to throw that rock.

1. What would you have said and done if you were James?

    _____
    _____
    _____

2. Have you ever been pressured by other kids to do something wrong? What kinds of things did they say and do to pressure you?

    _____
    _____
    _____

3. How did you react to the pressure? Did you go along with them or did you resist in some way?

    _____
    _____
    _____

4. Why do kids sometimes do things they know are wrong just because other kids want them to?

    _____
    _____
    _____

A Time I Said No
A Sharing Circle

Objectives:

The students will:
— describe what it is like to say no to a friend.
— affirm one another for having and exercising refusal skills.

Introduce the Topic:

Our topic today is, "A Time I Said No." As you think about this topic, focus on times you have said no to your peers. Try to recall a situation in which a friend asked you to do something that you didn't want to do — or maybe you did want to do it but knew it was wrong. Perhaps a friend asked you to give him the answers on a test or let him copy your homework. Or maybe someone asked you to lie for her, and say that she was with you when she wasn't. Maybe a friend offered you a cigarette or alcohol. Whatever it was, you said no. Tell us what happened and how you felt when you refused, but please don't mention any names. The topic is, "A Time I Said No."

Discussion Questions:

1. What does it take to say no to a friend?
2. Is it possible to say no to a friend without losing that person's friendship? How?
3. Have you ever said yes while wishing you had the guts to say no? What would have happened if you had said no?

What's Good and Bad About Peer Pressure

A Sharing Circle

Objectives:

The students will:
— define peer pressure.
— describe both positive and negative outcomes of peer pressure.

Introduce the Topic:

Usually we think of peer pressure as a bad thing — kids pressuring each other to do things like use drugs and join gangs. But today, we're going to talk about both sides of peer pressure, because there is a good side, too. Our topic is, "What's Good and Bad About Peer Pressure."

Tell us one thing that you think is bad about peer pressure, but also share one positive thing. If possible, draw from experiences with your own friends, but don't mention names. For example, maybe your peers have pressured you to take good risks, like running for school office or trying out for a team. On the other hand, they might have pressured you to take bad risks, like doing stunts on your skateboard that you're not skilled enough to do, or going somewhere after school that your parents have said is off limits. Peers can pressure you to use tobacco, alcohol, bad language, drugs, and to do lots of other undesirable things, but they can also pressure you to stay fit, dress nicely, use good manners, and participate in worthwhile activities. Take a minute to think about it. Our topic is, "What's Good and Bad About Peer Pressure."

Discussion Questions:

1. Who makes the final decision about what you will do and won't do?
2. Why is peer pressure so hard to resist?
3. What goes through your mind when you are deciding whether to go along with peer pressure or not?

Identifying Sources of Influence

Experience Sheet and Discussion

Objectives:
The students will:
— define the term influence.
— distinguish between positive and negative influence.
— identify people and things that influence them.

Materials:
one copy of the experience sheet, "Who Influences You" for each student; whiteboard

Procedure:

Begin by asking the students: What is *influence*?

Listen to and consider all suggestions, keeping notes on the board. Add components from the following definition to ensure student understanding.

An influence is something or someone that causes you to feel, think, or behave in a certain way without force or coercion.

Offer some examples:

All of your friends are wearing a certain style of clothes and shoes. The next time you shop for clothes and shoes you buy that style, too.

A speaker at a school assembly talks about the problem of disappearing landfills. You urge your family to start recycling aluminum, paper, and plastics.

The attractive woman on the TV commercial says your teeth will be whiter if you brush with Frostynut toothpaste. The next time you need toothpaste, you ask your mom to buy Frostynut.

Point out that influence sometimes causes people to do things, like buy a product. Other times it causes them to imitate someone — in appearance, speech, thought, or behavior. No matter how independent individuals are or how able to make their own decisions, they are still influenced to some degree by people and things outside themselves.

Next, help the students distinguish between positive and negative influences. In your own words, say: *Some people bring out our positive qualities, by setting a good example or expecting us to do our best. Other people have a negative influence on us. They have a way of bringing out our weaknesses.*

Finally, include in your discussion the form of influence known as *peer pressure*. Explain that peer pressure is a very strong form of influence. It isn't always bad, but very often it puts us in no-win positions. We don't know whether or not to do what the other person wants. If we *don't* do it, we may lose a friendship, and if we *do* we'll be going against ourselves. Either way, we lose — or so it seems.

Distribute the experience sheets and give the students a few minutes to complete them. Circulate and assist, as necessary.

Have the students share their completed experience sheets in groups of four. Lead a culminating class discussion.

Discussion Questions:

1. What similarities and differences did the members of your group see in the types of people who influence you?
2. Is there anyone or anything influencing you that you would like to reduce or eliminate? Explain.
3. What can you do to reduce the influence of someone or something?
4. What are some of positive things that can result from peer pressure? What are some negative things?

Who Influences You?
Experience Sheet

Who influences you?

Here is a list of people. Circle the ones who you believe have the most influence on you.

—a friend your age

—your next-door neighbor

—a movie star

—a political leader

—your minister, priest, or rabbi

—an adult friend

—an aunt, uncle, cousin, or grandparent

—a rock star

—a teacher

—a parent

—the principal of your school

—a brother or sister

—the star of a favorite TV show

Who else? Write their names here:

_____

_____

_____

Which people on your list usually have a *positive* influence on you and which ones usually have a *negative* influence? Mark them with a "P" or "N."

Choose Your Influences.
As much as possible, arrange to be around those people who influence you positively and stay away from those who influence you negatively.

Can you think of a time when you decided someone had the kind of influence on you that you valued?

Who was it? _____

_____

How did you allow yourself to be influenced by this person?

_____

_____

_____

Describe a time when you decided not to let someone influence you.

_____

_____

_____

What was your reason?

_____

_____

_____

What were some of the feelings you had?

_____

_____

The next time you're being pressured to do something you don't want to do or know is wrong, ask yourself this question:

Would a true friend constantly pressure me to do things I don't want to do?

Don't give in to people who put you in this kind of position. **SAY NO.**

Feel the Difference
Assertiveness Practice

Objectives:

The students will:
— nonverbally demonstrate three response styles — passive, aggressive, and assertive.
— describe feelings and consequences associated with the three response styles.
— practice responding assertively in specific situations.

Materials:

one copy of the response situations for each student or small group

Procedure:

On the board, write the following pairs of response roles:

<u>Passive</u> Polly
Wimpy Walter

<u>Aggressive</u> Anna
Demanding David

<u>Assertive</u> Sean
Confident Connie

Talk to the students about the differences between passive, aggressive, and assertive behaviors. For example, say:

Passive Polly rarely stands up for her own rights. She does whatever other people want her to do, even if it's wrong. Like Wimpy Walter, she slumps and slouches, and doesn't look people in the eye when she talks to them.

Aggressive Anna and Demanding David don't care about the feelings or rights of others. They just want to get their own way, even if they have to put other people down in the process. Aggressive Anna is often loud and sarcastic. Demanding David frequently gets into fights with other kids.

Assertive Sean and Confident Connie know how to stand up for their own rights and, at the same time, respect the rights of others. They don't let people talk them into doing things that are bad for them, and they take responsibility for their own actions. You can tell they feel good about themselves by the way they stand up straight and speak up clearly.

Ask two volunteers (a girl and a boy) to come to the front of the class and demonstrate the nonverbal attitudes and behaviors they would expect each pair of characters to exhibit. Get the class involved by asking: *What kind of facial expression would a Passive Polly have? How would Wimpy Walter stand? What are some gestures Demanding David might use? What kind of posture does Assertive Sean have? Etc.*

Ask the students to form groups of three. Have the members of each group divide the three response roles — passive, aggressive, and assertive — between them. Give each student (or each group) a copy of the response situations described on the next page.

Have the groups role play each situation three times, with each member of the group responding according to his/her role. Instruct them to switch response roles between situations, so that every member has a chance to practice all three response styles. When it is not their turn to respond to a situation, group members are to play the other roles in the scenario or act as "drama coach" to the responder. Encourage the students to get in touch with their feelings in each role, and to dramatically demonstrate the differences between the three styles.

Lead a culminating discussion to help them evaluate the experience.

Discussion Questions:

1. How did you feel when you were being passive? ...aggressive? ...assertive?
2. How did you feel when you were responded to passively? ...aggressively? ...assertively?
3. Why is assertive behavior less threatening to the other person than aggressive behavior?
4. What would happen if you were always passive? ...always aggressive?
5. How can a shy person learn to be more assertive? ...an aggressive person?

Variation:

Have the students write a 1-page story about one of the response roles (Passive Polly, Assertive Sean, etc.). Tell them to describe a situation (or use one of the situations listed here), how their character responds in the situation, and what happens as a result.

Response Situations

1. You and your friend have just come out of a movie and are met by your friend's older brother. He is supposed to drive you home. You can tell from his breath and his actions that he has been drinking. You whisper something about it to your friend, but your friend shrugs it off and heads for the car.

2. You are in a department store and have picked out something to buy. You stand in line at the cash register. When it is your turn, the clerk ignores you and helps the next adult in line.

3. You are riding in the back seat of a car on a freeway with all the windows rolled up. The adult in the front passenger's seat lights up a cigarette. In seconds the entire car is full of smoke and you start to feel sick.

Dozens of Ways to Say No

Brainstorming, Role Play and Discussion

Objectives:
The students will:
— distinguish between friendly and teasing forms of peer pressure.
— formulate and practice specific ways of saying no to peer pressure.

Materials:
chart paper or large sheets of butcher paper; marking pens

Procedure:

Have the students form groups of six to eight and choose a recorder. Give each group a sheet of chart or butcher paper.

Write the word, *friendly* on the board and draw a smiley face next to it. Remind the students that sometimes peer pressure comes in friendly forms — from kids they know and like. Perhaps the hardest thing about saying no to friendly pressure is the fear of hurting a relationship or losing a friend. But by saying no in a friendly way, the students can stand up for themselves while at the same time reassuring their friend that they like and value him or her. They may even influence their friend to say no, too. Offer some examples of friendly responses (see next page).

Tell the groups to write down as many friendly ways of saying no as they can brainstorm in 5 minutes. Circulate among the groups, randomly role-playing sources of friendly pressure by saying to individual students (for example): *Oh, don't worry, Karen it's only a little glass of beer.*

Next, write the word *teasing* on the board and draw a smirky face next to it. Remind the students that dares, bribes, put downs and other forms of teasing are also used to pressure us to do things we shouldn't do. One of the hardest things about saying no to teasing pressure is not wanting to look foolish, dumb, or weak. Learning "snappy" ways to say no can help. Offer some examples of snappy responses (next page).

Ask the groups to write down as many snappy ways of saying no as they can brainstorm in 5 minutes. Encourage them to have fun. Circulate and role play sources of teasing pressure, e.g.: *Hey, grow up Dave — are you always going to do what your mommy says?*

Have the groups take turns reading their friendly and snappy responses to the class. Then post the lists where everyone can see them.

Practice using the responses. Randomly approach different students and role play peer pressure situations, such as offering them alcohol and other drugs, or goading them into unethical or illegal acts. Vary your invitations from friendly to teasing. Have the students pick their responses from the posted lists. Encourage them to stand, and to use appropriate posture, gestures, facial expressions, volume, etc.

Conclude the activity with a general class discussion. Another ideal way to conclude this activity is to have the class sing the song, *I Can Say 'No! When I Want To*. You will need to improvise or borrow a tune prior to teaching the song, or the music is available as a download from www.songsforteaching.com. It can also be read as a poem.

Discussion Questions:

1. Why is it sometimes hard to say no to a friend?
2. If a friend gets mad at you when you say no, what can you do to feel better about it?
3. Why does it help to practice saying no in different ways?

Sample Friendly Responses
—No, I really don't want to.
—I'd like to go to your party, but if no adults are going to be there I can't.
—No thanks. Why don't we ride bikes instead.
—I don't want to mess up my mind, and I wish you wouldn't mess up yours either.
—No, I never put this body in dangerous situations. Let's think of something else to do.

Sample Snappy Responses
—No thanks, I'd rather walk my pet python.
—I'm not interested. I've got better things to do.
—No thanks. I like to get my bad breath from pepperoni pizza.
—Thanks, but if I'm going to ruin my body, I'll do it with a hot fudge sundae.
—No, but do you happen to have any milk? I'm on a program to build brain cells.

No! X 4 = Goodbye!

Discussion and Skill Development

Objectives:
The students will:
— learn four ways of saying no.
— practice using refusal skills to resist peer pressure.

Materials:
chart paper and markers or whiteboard; a watch or clock with a second hand

Procedure:
Remind the students of any previous discussions/activities related to peer pressure. Suggest that when they decide to resist peer pressure, the next big challenge is to say no. Saying no can be hard, particularly in the face of teasing, put-downs, promises, and threats.

Write these four methods of saying no on the board and discuss them with the students. Do a few quick role plays for practice.

1. Say no

No, thank you.

Say it politely, firmly, or any other way that fits the situation. If necessary, repeat it. Use the "broken record" technique.

2. Say no and give a reason.

No. I don't want to hurt my lungs.

Keep your explanation short. Remember, you have a right to make your own decision. You don't have to justify or defend yourself.

3. Say no and change the subject or suggest something else to do.

No thanks. Let's ride our bikes to the park.

Be assertive. Take charge of the situation. Do something you want to do.

4. Say no and leave.

No. (while walking away)

Use this method when the other three don't work. Always use this method with strangers or if you think you are in danger. Go immediately for help.

Point out that it pays to learn four different ways to say no because sometimes saying no once, or in just one way, doesn't work. Explain: *One reason saying no doesn't always work is that the person we are saying no to often doesn't accept our refusal. Instead, he or she keeps trying to convince us to do the thing we don't want to do. You've probably been in this sort of situation many times — trying to resist a brother, sister, or friend who pleads, argues, and tries to get you to change your mind. Act out a familiar example, such as one child persistently urging another to come over to his/her house.*

Ask the students to pair up and sit facing each other for a practice exercise. Have them decide who will be the Convincer and who will be the Resister in the first round. List several starter situations on chart paper or board, such as:
—Try some of these pills.
—Go to the movie I want to see.
—Let me copy your homework.
—Take out the trash for me.

Coach the Convincers to try anything they can think of to get a "yes" answer. Tell the Resisters to keep resisting, using any or all of the four methods. The livelier this exercise gets, the better. Encourage enthusiastic role playing. Allow at least 1 minute for each round. Then have the students switch roles and pick a new topic from the list.

Conclude the activity with a class discussion.

Discussion Questions:

1. How did you feel as the Convincer?
2. How did you feel when you were saying no?
3. Which method of saying no was easiest for you? Which was hardest?
4. Did you feel like you had to explain your reasons for saying no?
5. Did resisting get any easier as you continued to do it?

I CAN SAY "NO!"

(1) I can say "No" when I want to,
I can say "No" when I think I should.
I can say "No" when I want to,
I can say "No" when it's for my own good.
    Yeah, my friends may laugh and call me names,
    But it's my life, not theirs, I claim,
I'll say "No" when I want to,
I'll say "No" when I think I should!

(2) I can say "No" when I want to,
I can say "No" when I think I should.
I can say "No" when I want to,
I can say "No" when it's for my own good.
    If everybody's doing it, just the same,
    That doesn't mean I've got to play their game.
I'll say "No" when I want to,
I'll say "No" when I think I should!

(3) I can say "No" when I want to,
I can say "No" when I think I should.
I can say "No" when I want to,
I can say "No" when it's for my own good.
    I want them all to like me, that's for sure,
    Being true to myself has got to be worth more.
I'll say "No" when I want to,
I'll say "No" when I think I should!

(4) I can say "No" when I want to,
I can say "No" when I think I should.
I can say "Unh-uh" when I want to,
I can say "Naw" when it's for my own good.
    If I don't like where they're leading, I won't follow like a lamb;
    I'll make my own decisions and stand by them,
And say "No" when I want to,
I'll say "No" when I think I should!

(5) I can say "No" — "Nah" — when I want to,
I can say "Hunh-uh" when I think I should.
I can say "No-o-o way!"
I can say "Unh!" — it's for my own good.
    If I don't like where they're leading, I won't follow...
    I'll just make my own decisions
And say "No" when I want to,
I'll say "No" when I think I should!

(6) I can say "No-o-o way!"
I can say "Unh-uh,"
I can say "Unh — No!"
I can say "Mmmmh-mm!"
    If I don't like where they're leading, I won't follow...
    I'll make my own decisions
And say "No" — "Uh, unh-uh" when I want to,
I'll say "No" when I think I should!

Music is available, as a download, from www.songsforteaching.com

Copyright 1996 by Linda K. Williams

Ethical Decision Making

Story:
Midnight Decision
Experience Sheet

Sharing Circles:
A Time I Stood Up for What Was Right
A Time I Told the Truth Even Though It Hurt

Activities:
Sign Up for Ethics
Bingo Game and Discussion

Against the Wall!
Decision Making and Discussion

Putting Moral Values First
Experience Sheet and Discussion

Making Ethical Choices
Dyad Decision Making and Discussion

Song/Poem:
What Should I Do?

Midnight Decision
by Tom Pettepiece

Julie invited thirty-five girls to a slumber party Saturday night! Her mother couldn't believe it. Thirty-five! And they all said they would come!

The big farm house would hold them all, counting the living room, family room, Julie's bedroom, Mike's room (her brother was gone for the weekend), and the hallways, if everyone brought sleeping bags. "That's the fun of it, Mom," Julie pleaded. "These are the neatest girls in school. And besides, they're all my friends."

By joining the girls chorus, Julie had made a lot of new friends. Her mother had met most of them at one time or another when Julie brought them home after school or when they needed a ride to the movies. They did seem like nice girls. As she looked into her daughter's hopeful eyes, Julie's mother remembered her own lonely childhood growing up in the country, far from kids her own age. Julie, too, lived a pretty isolated life on this farm where the family grew vegetables for a living. The least she could do was let her daughter have a party for her friends.

"Okay," she said, grinning. "I'm sure we'll manage."

Julie screamed. "Really? Great Mom! Thank you so much. We'll be soooo good."

On Friday night all thirty-five girls showed up, drank gallons of punch, ate tons of chips and hot dogs, and practically brought the roof down yelling during games and dancing to loud rock music. Good thing they lived on a farm!

Fortunately for Julie's mother, only about half of the girls could stay over. At 10 p.m., the girls remaining vowed to stay up all night talking or die in the attempt.

Julie looked around at the group lying on the living room rug with pillows scattered all over, and thought it seemed smaller than it should be. A moment later, Julie noticed several girls walking by the partially open front door. Getting up, she hollered at them, "Hey, where are you going?"

No one spoke. Then Clara said, "We're going to the party at Darcie's. It's kinda boring here."

Feeling hurt, but not wanting to offend her friends or have them think she was bossy, Julie said, "Great, okay, fine. Ah... but come back soon, okay?"

"Yeah, okay," was the reluctant reply.

Two hours later, at midnight, Julie heard loud singing coming from the driveway. The wayward girls had returned — drunk out of their minds. Julie knew Darcie drank. In fact, most of the kids who went to those parties drank. That's why she was pleased that everyone had come to her house instead.

"Great, you guys," she said upon meeting the group in the driveway. "Shh. My Mom'll hear you. Shut-up!"

"Shut-up yourself, Miss Priss," one of them said. "Who made you our guardian angel?"

"Go inside with your pajama party, little girl. I don't know why we came back here anyway, girls. Let's go back to Darcie's."

By now Julie was mad. Not only had these girls insulted her and caused a commotion, they'd used Julie as an excuse to go to Darcie's party.

"Go ahead. I don't care," she said firmly. "But if you're not back by two o'clock, don't bother coming back, because I'm locking the door."

One girl shouted obscenities at Julie. The rest only grumbled as they stormed off through the dark to Darcie's.

In the back bedroom, Julie's mother closed the drapes over a corner of the window bordering the driveway. She had witnessed the entire scene.

Eight-thirty a.m. No one moved. The last eyelid had closed about four o'clock, and now the entire group of sleeping girls looked like one massive blanket covering the floor. The ringing phone that woke them sounded like a burglar alarm going off next to their ears. Julie stumbled to the kitchen.

"Hello," said the cheerful woman's voice. "Is Katie there'?"

"Katie who?" Julie mumbled, still half asleep.

"Katie Mullens," the voice said. "It's her mother."

Julie started awake. Her eyes popped open as she remembered that Katie was one of the group that had gone off to Darcie's. No one had seen them since. "Uh," she muttered. "Just a moment."

Julie's mom emerged from the bedroom, and sensed what was happening. Holding her hand over the receiver, Julie said to her mom, "What am I going to do? Katie's not here and her mom wants to speak to her."

"Is she one of the ones who was drinking last night?"

Julie looked stunned. "How...?"

"I saw what happened, and heard what you told them. You handled it quite well."

Relieved, Julie responded. "Uh ... thanks, Mom. But what do I tell Katie's mother?"

"How about the truth?"

"Do you know what Katie and her friends will do to me if I don't cover for them? I won't have a friend left at school."

"No one ever said growing up would always be easy, Julie," her mother said, "but you must do what's right."

Julie gulped. "Mrs. Mullen?" she finally said. "Katie isn't here. She and some of the girls went to Darcie's about midnight and haven't been back since."

Silence. Mrs. Mullen didn't speak for a long time. "Oh," she finally aid, "I see. Thank you," and she hung up.

As the day wore on, additional phone calls began coming in from parents of the girls who'd gone to Darcie's party. Pretty soon everyone found out that Julie had told the truth. All the parents were angry, but not all at their daughters. Some ranted at Julie's mother for allowing the girls to leave. Others called Julie a liar, saying their daughters told them they didn't go to Darcie's and that they didn't drink.

By the following day, not only were all the girls who had been drinking mad at Julie, several of her other friends were as well. They called her a narc, a fink, a traitor and worse. Julie felt miserable and sad. She told the director of girls chorus that she was quitting.

Two nights later, the choral director phoned and spoke to first Julie, then her parents.

"I wanted you to know that I understand why you'd want to quit the chorus with the other girls rejecting you like they did," she said to Julie. "What you did took a lot of courage."

"Thanks, but a lot of good it did," Julie said. "A bunch of girls drink at parties but don't tell their parents. Now they're mad at me for telling on them, and a lot of their parents think I'm a liar besides! I'd just rather forget it."

"Well, I wouldn't," said the director. "Your real friends haven't forgotten," she said. Julie was puzzled. "It seems that about ten of them have also decided to quit the chorus if you aren't going to be in it. By saying no and telling the truth, you may have started something."

Feeling better, Julie said, "Yeah, like finding out that the quality of my friendships is more important than the quantity."

"Something like that," the director said.

Within a week, Julie rejoined the chorus, supported by her true friends. One by one, the other girls dropped out when it became clear to them that drinking — and drinkers — were not welcome in the chorus.

Discussion Questions:

1. Why did Julie have such a big slumber party?
2. Were Clara and the other girls who went to Darcie's party showing respect for Julie and her family? Explain.
3. Why did Clara and the other girls take advantage of Julie?
4. Should Julie have stopped the girls from going to Darcie's? How could she have done so?
5. Why was telling the truth difficult for Julie? Why was it the right thing to do?
6. What affect did Julie's decision to lock the girls out have on them? What other ways could she have handled the situation?
7. What should Julie's Mom have done when she discovered what was happening? Why did she decide not to interfere?
8. Why did Julie quit the chorus? What would you have done?

Midnight Decision
Experience Sheet

Think about the story of Julie and her friends at the slumber party. Remember as much of the story as you can. Then answer these questions:

1. Several difficult decisions were made by the people in this story? What were they?

   _____
   _____
   _____
   _____
   _____

2. If you had to make decisions like these, how would you go about it? (Suggestion: Take one decision from your list and think it through..)

   _____
   _____
   _____

3. Think of a tough decision you had to make. Write about it here:

   _____
   _____
   _____
   _____
   _____

A Time I Stood Up for What Was Right
A Sharing Circle

Objectives:
The students will:
— distinguish between right and wrong choices in situations involving others.
— identify specific benefits that resulted from ethical decisions.

Introduce the Topic:

Today we're going to talk about situations that require courage, the courage to do what is right when our companions are doing — or are about to do — something wrong. Our topic is, "A Time I Stood Up for What Was Right."

Think about situations in which you were with other people — kids or family members — and something happened that caused you to take a stand. Maybe a friend wanted to do something dishonest or hurtful, and you refused to be involved. Perhaps some kids wanted to go somewhere that was unsafe or off-limits, and you talked them out of it. Or maybe you convinced a friend, or a brother or sister, to tell the truth instead of lying. Without mentioning any names, tell us what happened and how you felt. The topic is, "A Time I Stood Up for What Was Right."

Discussion Questions:

1. What is courage? How did we get up our courage in the situations we talked about?
2. How do you feel inside when you stand up for the right thing?
3. How were the other people in our examples better off because we took a stand? How did they benefit?

A Time I Told the Truth Even Though It Hurt

A Sharing Circle

Objectives:

The students will:
— describe situations in which they accepted the consequences of their actions.
— identify truth-telling as a basic moral value.
— state the benefits of being honest.

Introduce the Topic:

Have you ever heard someone say, "The truth hurts?" Well, the truth can hurt sometimes. The truth can be painful to tell, and it can also be painful to hear. However, usually the hurt only lasts a short time, while the good that comes from telling the truth can last a long time. We're going to talk about examples of difficult truth-telling today. Our topic is, "A Time I Told the Truth Even Though It Hurt."

Think of a time when being honest was tough, but you were honest anyway. Maybe you broke a rule at home, and when your parent asked about it you confessed — even though you knew you'd be punished. Perhaps a friend asked you if you liked something and you answered honestly, even though it made your friend sore at you for a little while. Or maybe instead of pretending to the teacher that you completed your reading assignment, you admitted you didn't. Do you tell the truth when your parent asks if you've finished your homework, even though it means no TV? Rather than making up some flimsy excuse, have you ever admitted that you stayed out past your deadline because you wanted to? Telling the truth and accepting the consequences makes us better people. Think of a time you had the courage to be honest. The topic is, "A Time I Told the Truth Even Though It Hurt."

Discussion Questions:

1. How did you feel when you were telling the truth? How did you feel afterwards?
2. Why do you think people lie?
3. Why is it important to accept the consequences of our actions?
4. What would it be like if everyone lied to protect themselves and you could never count on anyone to tell the truth?

Sign Up for Ethics!
Bingo Game and Discussion

Objectives:
The students will:
—acknowledge each other and themselves for ethical behaviors.
—identify specific behaviors associated with four universal moral values.

Materials:
one copy of the "Ethics Bingo!" experience sheet and a pen or pencil for each student

Procedure:
Use this activity as a warm-up or energizer, and to help the students focus on ethical behavior in the context of four universal moral values — honesty, respect, responsibility, and kindness.

Distribute the bingo sheets and explain to the students that they are to mill about, interviewing their classmates, in an effort to find someone to sign each square on their sheet.

Depending on the size of the group, limit the number of times a particular student's signature may appear on each sheet. For example, if ten students are playing, you may wish to allow students to sign the same sheet up to three times. If twenty are playing, the limit might be two times; thirty might be limited to one signing per sheet.

Instruct the students to talk to each other about the items on their sheets. For example, if a student says she "did a favor for someone recently," find out what the favor was and for whom it was done.

Give a prize or privilege to the first student to accurately complete the sheet.

Conclude the activity with a follow-up discussion.

Discussion Questions:
1. Were any squares particularly hard to fill? Which ones?
2. Which squares were the easiest to fill?
3. What are ethics?
4. What is one word that describes all of the behaviors listed on the sheet?
5. Do you think it's possible to learn to do all of these things, all of the time? Why or why not?

Variation:
Distribute the bingo sheets, but instead of having the students fill them out in class, stipulate that they may be completed only during recess and lunch breaks. Give the students one or two days to get their signatures.

Ethics Bingo!
Experience Sheet

Get someone to sign your sheet who:

Respect	Kindness
says "please" and "thank you"	hugged someone today
says "excuse me"	appreciates others
is a good listener	did a favor for someone recently
is usually on time	writes letters to friends or relatives
settles conflicts peacefully	complimented someone today
throws away litter	makes cards or gifts to give to others
accepts people's differences	calls a grandparent just to say hello
Honesty	**Responsibility**
returned a lost item	cares for a pet
hasn't cheated on a test this year	makes own bed
tells the truth	always follows rules and obeys laws
kept a promise this week	is a good role model for younger children
stands up for friends and family	did all his/her homework this week
never asks a friend to do something wrong	admits mistakes
always returns borrowed things	controls his/her temper

Against the Wall!
Decision Making and Discussion

Objectives:
The students will:
— evaluate their own and others' behavior.
— share and discuss different perceptions of the same behavior.
— discuss how values and ethics are formed.
— explain the difference between thinking about and doing something bad.

Materials:
whiteboard; three signs prepared prior to the session (see "Procedure")

Procedure:
Ask the students if they know what the term *ethics* means. Write the word on the board, listen to any ideas that the students voice, and clarify that ethics are principles or values having to do with right and wrong.

Ask the students: *Who can tell us about something you've done in the last few days that was a good thing to do?*

Call on volunteers. After each person shares, ask him or her: *How did you know that what you did was a good thing to do?*

Discuss various ways of knowing: because it feels good, because parents have said it's good, because anything else would feel bad, etc.

Next, ask the students: *Who is willing to tell us about a bad thing you've done recently?*

Again, ask each volunteer: *How do you know that what you did was bad?*

Be sure to take a turn yourself and share something that you're not proud of having done. Emphasize that all people do bad things at times. That doesn't mean that they are bad people, only that they made a mistake. The most important thing is to recognize and admit that you've done something wrong and learn from the experience.

Place these three signs (prepared ahead of time) on the wall:

- I think that was a very good thing to do.
- I'm not sure whether it was good or bad.
- I think that was a very bad thing to do.

Tell the students that you are going to read them some situations. They are to go and stand in front of the sign that matches what they think or feel about the behavior of the <u>principal person</u> in the situation.

One at a time, read the situations from the list on the following page. Give the students time to decide and position themselves. Then walk up to each group and ask individual students, "Why are you standing here?"

Interview the students about their reasons for deciding the way the did. Underscore examples that demonstrate different perceptions of what happened in the situation. When values have played a clear role in someone's decision, discuss with the class how values are developed.

Have the students return to their seats. Conclude the activity with a general discussion.

Discussion Questions:

1. What's the difference between having a bad thought or feeling, and actually doing a bad thing?
2. When you find yourself thinking about doing something bad, how do you stop yourself from doing it?
3. How do we learn the difference between good and bad, right and wrong?
4. If you know that a friend is about to do something bad, should you try to stop him or her? Why or why not?
5. How about just saying, "It's not my problem" and not worrying about it?

Extension:

Consider spreading the various parts of this activity over two or three days. Then spend more time examining each part: good behaviors; bad behaviors; the role of values and perceptions; the differences between thinking/feeling and doing; and how ethics are developed.

Situations:

- Keith beats up a younger boy because he overhears the boy call his sister a bad name.

- Without asking, Maria borrows an old ring of her mother's. When she loses it, Maria decides not to say anything. Chances are her mother won't notice that the ring is missing for a long, long time.

- Omar is in a big hurry to get home. He can't see any cars in either direction so he crosses on the red signal.

- Serena sees a girl she doesn't like cheating on a spelling test, so she tells the teacher.

- Linda sees her friend cheating on a social studies quiz, and doesn't say anything to anyone.

- Sandie overhears the teacher scolding two classmates for leaving a mess on the work table. Sandie helped make the mess, but she doesn't speak up.

- Three tough kids are making fun of a new student. Reginald is a little afraid of the tough kids, but he stands up for the new student anyway, telling the tough kids to get lost.

- Jon stays up very late watching old movies and can barely move the next morning. He decides to stay home from school and get some sleep.

- Roberto finishes his homework early, so he helps his younger brother with his homework.

- Jeanne knows that Mr. Snipes hates to have kids cut across his lawn, but she also knows that Mr. Snipes is on vacation, so she cuts across anyway.

I think that was a very bad thing to do.

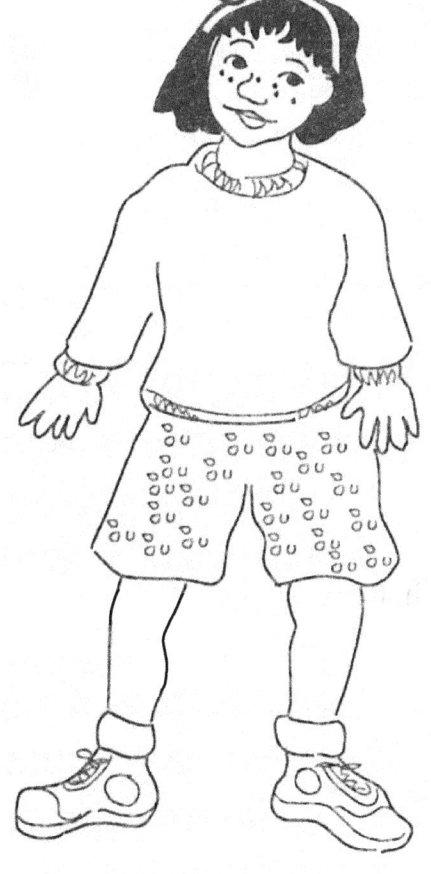

Making Ethical Choices
Dyad Decision Making and Discussion

Objectives:
The students will:
— define six core universal moral values.
— identify the stakeholders in situations involving core values.
— learn and practice a decision-making process for making ethical choices.

Materials:
whiteboard; writing materials for the students

Procedure:
Write the following core universal moral values on the board and talk about their meaning:

Trustworthiness (Honesty)
Respect
Responsibility
Kindness
Justice/Fairness
Citizenship

Tell the students that these core moral values always take precedence over other values when decisions about ethical conduct are made. Point out that occasionally an ethical decision will seem to pit one core value against another; for example, honesty against kindness. In cases like these it is helpful to follow these decision-making steps (list steps on board):

1. Identify all of the stakeholders in the situation. (A stakeholder is any person who will be directly or indirectly affected by the decision.)

2. Brainstorm possible courses of action. List them.

3. Determine which core values are involved in each possible course of action.

4. Determine how each course of action will affect the various stakeholders.

5. Decide which, if any, core values are in conflict.

6. Make a decision. When core values are in conflict, follow the core value that provides the greatest good (or is good for the most stakeholders).

Read one of the following situations slowly to the class. Wait a moment and then read it a second time. Lead the class in following the decision-making steps as a group. On the board list stakeholders, possible courses of action, and the core values of each course of action. Decide which core values are in conflict. Discuss affects on stakeholders, etc. Finally, make a decision for the "greatest good."

Ask the students to form pairs. Read them a second situation and have the partners go through the same decision-making process together, making their lists and notes on paper.

After each situation, ask the groups to report their decision and reasoning to the class. Ask the questions (below) and facilitate discussion before reading aloud the next situation.

Wrap up the discussion by singing the song, "What Should I Do?" Prior to teaching the song, borrow or compose a simple tune to fit the lyrics. The words may also be read as a poem.

Discussion Questions:

1. What stakeholders did you list?
2. What core moral values did you identify?
3. Which, if any, core values are in conflict in this situation?
4. What alternative courses of action did you identify?
5. What is your final course of action in this situation? Why is it the best choice?

Situations:

- If Sara doesn't get a B or better in Social Studies on her report card, her parents will make her quit the soccer team. Sara is a great goalie and the team needs her. Sara considers cheating on the final Social Studies test. She tells herself she will be doing it for the team.

Stakeholders: Sara, team members, teacher, other students, parents
Core Values in Conflict: Trustworthiness and Fairness vs. Responsibility (to team)

- Kim's grandmother is always giving the family rhubarb pies that she makes herself. No one in the family likes rhubarb, but no one wants to be the one to break the news to grandmother. When asked if she liked the latest pie, Kim tells her grandmother, "yes," because she doesn't want to hurt her feelings.

Stakeholders: Kim, grandmother, other family members
Core Values in Conflict: Trustworthiness and Respect vs. Kindness

- Gary is entering the 7th grade, but his parents don't like the middle school he's supposed to attend. Gary's aunt lives several miles away and they think the middle school in her neighborhood is much better, so they consider using her address to enroll Gary there.

Stakeholders: Gary, parents, aunt, other students at both schools, parents of other students at both schools, teachers at both schools
Core Values in Conflict: Responsibility and Kindness (to Gary) vs. Trustworthiness (including modeling honesty for Gary), Citizenship and Responsibility (to schools and community)

- Julie's mother never lets her attend the birthday parties of her friends. So when Victoria's party comes up, Julie tells her mom that she is going to Victoria's to work on a school project. All the other girls agree to cover for Julie if anyone asks them.

Stakeholders: Julie, other girls, mother, parents of other girls
Core Values in Conflict: Trustworthiness vs. Fairness

Putting Moral Values First
Experience Sheet and Discussion

Objectives:
The students will:
— explain the concept of self-interest.
— prescribe ethical behaviors for typical self-interest situations.
— identify the underlying moral values in each situation.

Materials:
one copy of the experience sheet, "Decision Point," for each small group; pencils/pens

Procedure:
Introduce the concepts of *self-interest* and *self-protection*. Point out that most of us know the difference between right and wrong. We often know exactly what we *should* do in a situation, even though we don't always do it. When we desire something for ourselves, we often let that desire get into a fight with our knowledge about what is right and wrong. Sometimes self-interest wins.

Have the students form groups of four or five. Give each group a copy of the experience sheet and go over the directions. In your own words, elaborate:

Take turns reading the situations aloud in your group. After a situation is read, brainstorm ideas about what the person in the situation should do. Have a recorder write down all the ideas. When the group runs out of ideas, go around the circle and take turns saying what you as an individual would do if you were in that situation.

In a follow-up discussion, focus on the moral values underlying each situation. Emphasize that when these moral values get into contests with self-interest, the moral values should always be the winners. Do not equivocate on this point.

Discussion Questions:
1. Which moral value are you breaking when you steal? (Honesty)
2. What moral values are you breaking if you treat someone badly just because he or she is different? (Respect/Kindness)
3. What moral values are you breaking when you keep something that doesn't belong to you? (Honesty/Responsibility)
4. What moral value are you breaking if you blame someone else (or allow someone to get blamed) for something you did? (Honesty/Responsibility/Respect)
5. Why are decisions like these sometimes hard to make?
6. How does making the right decisions help you become a good person?

Decision Point!
Experience Sheet

Take one situation at a time. Read it aloud and talk about it with your group. Make a list of the things you think the person in the situation *should* do. Then go around the group and take turns answering the question, "What would *you* do?"

1. Norman likes many toys, especially cars. At the toy store, he sees a car he has wanted for a long time, but it costs too much money. He looks around and sees that no one is watching. He could easily slip the car into his pocket. *What should Norman do?*

2. Lisa comes out to lunch late and sees her friends making fun of a new girl. Lisa likes the new girl and thinks that her friends should not make fun of her just because she is new. She wants to be with her friends because she likes them, but doesn't like to be mean. *What should Lisa do?*

3. Trahn finds a wallet on the ground. Inside is a twenty dollar bill — just enough money to buy his mother something nice for her birthday. Trahn knows he should return the wallet, but he wants to surprise his mom. *What should Trahn do?*

4. Shelly cracks the glass on her mother's computer monitor. She cracks it with her little sister's bat, which she isn't supposed to be using in the house. If she gets in trouble she won't be able to go to her friend's birthday party. She could easily blame it on her sister. *What should Shelly do?*

5. Eric's mom made a tray of fresh brownies. Those are Eric's favorite. His mom says that Eric can have only two. When Eric finishes his two brownies, he sees the plate sitting on the counter by itself and his mom isn't around. Eric really wants more brownies. *What should Eric do?*

6. Rosa and her best friend get in a fight. Rosa really wants to make up, but her friend won't talk to her. Rosa knows that she did something mean and wants to apologize, but her friend did something mean, too. *What should Rosa do?*

WHAT SHOULD I DO?

What should I do? Oh, what should I do?
There are so many choices, and consequences, too!
What to do with my money, how to spend my time,
Who to choose as my friends — oh, which choice should be mine?

I had so many decisions,
I didn't know how I could cope;
Then I learned some steps that cleared my head
And really gave me some hope.

So every problem that's bugging me,
I'll tackle it "1-2-3" —
I'll have some others think it through with me;
Two heads can be better than one, you see?

    (spoken) 1ST STEP: OPTIONS!
Well, what is the problem and what are my options?
Brainstorming gives me "umpteen" possible solutions!
—Got to step back, look at it inside-outside-upside-down!
People with experience can help take away my frown.

    (spoken) 2ND STEP: ACTION!
For each possible solution that I'd seriously consider,
I'll picture in my mind what would happen if I did it;
What are all the pro's and con's of the options I have found?
If the list's a long one, I might even write it down?

    (spoken) 3RD STEP: ACTION!
After lots of careful thinking, now I'm ready to make a choice.
The responsibility's scary, but I'm glad I had a voice.
So, with everything considered, I will choose the "best" solution,
Hope I've chosen wisely, and then put it into motion.

So now...
I know what to do, yes, I know what to do,
Though there are so many choices, and consequences, too.
And now I know how to think it through.
I might make a mistake or two,
But that's okay; the best of us do.
And now that I've decided what to do,
I feel a lot better.

    Music is available, as a download, from www.songsforteaching.com

Copyright 1996 by Linda K. Williams

If your heart is in Social-Emotional Learning, visit us online.

Come see us at
www.InnerchoicePublishing.com

Our web site gives you a look at all our other Social-Emotional Learning-based books, free activities, articles, research, and learning and teaching strategies. Every week you'll get a new Sharing Circle topic and lesson.

INNERCHOICE Publishing
15079 Oak Chase Court
Wellington, FL 33414

www.ingramcontent.com/pod-product-compliance
Lightning Source LLC
Chambersburg PA
CBHW080544170426
43195CB00016B/2674